To Ruth + Bob

Making the
Second Half
the Best Half

with love

from

Ed + Olive

Making the Second Half the Best Half

EDMUND · JANSS

BETHANY HOUSE PUBLISHERS
MINNEAPOLIS, MINNESOTA 55438
A Division of Bethany Fellowship, Inc.

Scripture quotations marked KJV are taken from the King James
Version of the Bible.

Verses marked TLB are taken from The Living Bible, copyright 1971 by
Tyndale House Publishers, Wheaton, IL. Used by permission.

Published by Bethany House Publishers
A Division of Bethany Fellowship, Inc.
6820 Auto Club Road, Minneapolis, MN 55438

Printed in the United States of America

Library of Congress Cataloging in Publication Data

Janss, Edmund W.
    Making the second half the best half.

    Bibliography: p.
    Includes index.
    1. Aged—Psychology.   2. Aging—Psychological
aspects.   I. Title.
HQ1061.J36   1984   305.2'6   83-15779
ISBN 0-87123-404-1

Dedication

To my sister, Helen Locklin,
who is making the second half of
her life better all the time.

Acknowledgments

Warm appreciation is expressed to these dear friends who helped
with the manuscript of this book:
    Dr. Donald Sapp
    Georgia Nelson
    Terri Owen
    and Olive, my wife.

EDMUND W. JANSS is Minister of Adults at the Paradise Valley United Methodist Church in Arizona. Previously he was Director of Childcare for World Vision, International, as well as Assistant Director of Christian Children's Fund, Inc. For fifteen years he also pastored churches in the Northeast and South.

Dr. Janss has traveled continuously to over fifty countries during the administration of his duties for the past quarter of a century. He holds the Ph.D. degree from New York University along with advanced degrees from Eastern Baptist Theological Seminary and Temple University.

He is the author of five books including the best-selling *Yankee Si!* which he wrote jointly with the late Dr. Daniel A. Poling, longtime editor of *Christian Herald* magazine.

Dr. and Mrs. Janss live in Fountain Hills, Arizona (a suburb of Phoenix) and are the parents of four grown children.

Foreword

Of all the books my friend of many years, Dr. Ed Janss, has written, this to me is one of the most helpful and contemporary pieces of writing to come from his heart and experience. Of all people, Christians should know how to plan so that "the second half can be the better half." We need to prove to those around us that "the path of the just is as the shining light, that shineth more and more unto the perfect day" (Prov. 4:18, KJV). This book will help us. It discloses many of the secrets for keeping active, creative, happy and young all our days.

Throughout their exceedingly busy, productive lives—and more particularly during this second half—Ed and Olive Janss have demonstrated the truths set forth here. While reading the manuscript, I was impressed again with the fact that we need to know and apply the principles for quality living which Dr. Janss has worked through with such care and discernment. I heartily commend the book to all who are approaching or making their pilgrimage into retirement.

Dr. Carlton Booth, Secretary-Treasurer
World Vision, Inc.
Monrovia, California

Contents

Introduction / Keep Young

Most of us go through life unaware of our body's slow aging—until we feel a sudden twinge, ache or pain. Inwardly we somehow visualize ourselves as eternally eighteen or twenty-one, even though the stairs seem a little steeper now, and the newsprint isn't as clear as it used to be.

A nineteenth-century author describes this process in his autobiography, telling of a visit to a house he had known in former years:

"At first I could not understand why I found some difficulty in recognizing the master of the house and the guests, and why everyone was made up—a makeup that usually included powder and altered them entirely. The prince had provided himself with a white beard and, as it were, lead soles which dragged at his feet. A name was mentioned to me, and I was dumbfounded at the thought that it applied to the blonde, vivacious girl I had once known, who was now the white-haired lady walking just in front of me. We did not see our own appearances, our own age, but each, like a facing mirror, saw the other's."

Basically we face two critical junctures in life—that of growing into adulthood and that of growing old. Each of these we must face with an affirming yes! Some people do, some do not. Some angry older folk cannot accept their ebbing vigor. They are the ones who usually could not accept an active challenge even before age faced them. They were grumblers from the beginning—about taxes, about children, about government, about an uncertain future. They *can* change, of course, but often do not.

We usually imagine youth in terms of flexibility, spontaneity, health, agility, creativity and a host of characteristics which we will discuss in this book. However, such virtues need not be confined only to the chronologically young. We discover in the Bible that "Moses was 120 years old when he died, yet his eyesight was perfect, and he was as strong as a young man." Most of us may not be that strong or sight-perfect, yet God's Word and His laws encourage us to live youthfully to the end of our earthly days.

To many people, the age 65 once meant we were "used up," and 75 meant we had one foot in the grave. But according to insurance tables, the average person at 65 can expect at least 16 additional active years. Age should remain a relative term. For example, baseball players are often considered old at 35, while basketball guards are "aged" at 30. Yet even these men can defy the averages by staying fit and young at heart. Ty Cobb at 42 was still a baseball star, and George Blanda played professional football until he was 48.

Medical studies tell us to "run and not rest." The body tends to rust out, not wear out. But there are fitness rules we will examine in depth throughout this volume.

I will always remember the little eighty-year-old lady who jogged every morning in my hometown. As I drove by, she waved at me and threw kisses. Looking in the car mirror, I could still see her throwing kisses to the cars that followed. She was affirming her life—at eighty years young!

On the other hand, there is the apocryphal epitaph presumably found on a country gravestone:

DIED AT FIFTY
BURIED AT SEVENTY
DEAD OF HARDENING OF VIEWPOINTS

So there are basic principles to staying young all your life which we intend to explore at length.

1. *Never give up*

Our entire period of growth, through youth and middle age, is a preparatory school for retirement. Whatever we do and believe about ourselves during those years lays the groundwork for our accomplishments in later life.

Winston Churchill, at sixty-two, was first elected as Prime Minister of Great Britain during England's darkest hour. After his election he said, "I felt as if I were walking with destiny and that all my past life had been but a preparation for this hour and this trial."

Much later, Churchill (by then in his eighties) was invited to speak at Harrow, his boyhood grammar school from which he had been graduated some seventy years before. There was a rustle of anticipation among the boys when he rose to speak, and then a breathless quiet. One of the modern masters of eloquence was about to address them.

With a stern countenance, Churchill looked out over his young audience and said, "Young men, never give up! Never give up! Never! Never! Never!" And then he sat down.

The youngsters were stunned. But he had given his whole autobiography to them in a few words. Perseverance was the keynote of his entire life. Even his famous portrait at Westminster depicts him as a veritable bulldog of a man.

Recently this letter to a physician appeared in our morning newspaper: "After forty years of hard work, my father retired; one year later he was dead of a heart attack. Although his work was physically hard, he had enjoyed it more than the year of retirement which he seemed unable to cope with. I'm beginning to think that if he had continued to work, he would still be alive today. Does this make sense from a medical standpoint?"

It is probably premature to come to a firm conclusion, but there is some evidence that retirement followed by idleness may in fact predispose one to a fatal heart attack. The apparent link between the two was identified by Dr. Charles H. Hennekens and his associates at the Harvard Medical School. More studies at Duke University are shedding additional light on the subject.

Paul Tournier tells of a Pastor Bremond who had a parish near Lyons, France. "Almost all my parishioners worked on the railroad," he told Dr. Tournier. "They were proud of being able to retire at fifty-five but they did not seem to notice that very few survived retirement by more than two years!"

Homes for the aged seem to have the same effect. Forty-nine percent of men and forty-four percent of women admitted into aged persons' institutions die within the first six months. Fortunately less than six percent of our elderly are confined to nursing homes.

2. *Plan ahead*

Studies indicate that as we become elderly we usually behave the way we did in youth and middle age—only more so. When someone has been generous in his early years, he becomes more giving as he grows older. The stubborn man frequently becomes a dictator. The namby-pamby becomes a dishrag.

Simone de Beauvior says, "Those who have already chosen mediocrity will not have much difficulty in fitting themselves in, and trimming their lives." But for advice on how to continue a productive life, listen to Drs. Ted Engstrom and Ed Dayton, in their fine book, *Strategy for Living*. They suggest four steps we should take toward meaningful life-plans:

a. Identify or write out your goals.
b. Describe your problem.
c. List the opposing forces in favor of and against your goals.
d. List the specific steps you plan to take toward your goals.

Your present lifestyle has already begun to lay the forms for your retirement days. Even though you do not know it, you have begun casting the mold of your old age.

Short courses on How to Retire are now being offered, covering such matters as health, legal, budgetary, social and spiritual issues of retirement. Without this type of planning, either formal or informal, a person's life may wander off into meaningless malaise—and possibly early death.

I once paid a visit to a beloved friend in his early sixties just before he retired. He had no special goals for his latter years beyond "taking it easy." He sold a successful business and never visited it again. He hated reading—other than the sports page. He and his wife traveled, but he didn't especially enjoy it. He stayed home, watched TV and dabbled in housework—to his wife's distress. His children were married with lives of their own. When I again visited him two years later, he was a shadow of his former self. He seemed to have aged twenty years. Shrunken and shriveled, he walked hesitantly—although only in his mid-sixties. His voice had the querulous pitch of a man in his nineties. And in another year he was dead.

The Apostle Paul indicated that he had maintained clear life-goals throughout his Christian life. He wrote them to Timothy from the Mammertine dungeons at Rome shortly before he was martyred: "I have fought a good fight, I have finished my course,

I have kept the faith" (2 Tim. 4:7, KJV). He planned his life and he kept his plans.

3. *Stay spontaneous*

One of the traits of youth is its spontaneity. Although it seems to be paradoxically opposed to planning, both traits can and should be maintained. I have watched many older men and women, now retired, who are both planned *and* spontaneous and enjoy every moment.

Some of the happiest times of my own married life (at age sixty-five) have been totally spontaneous. One day recently I was getting ready to fly to Los Angeles where I was scheduled to speak at a conference. Suddenly I said to my wife, "Why don't you come with me?" At first horrified, she protested, "But the plane leaves in two hours and I haven't packed!" "You pack," I said, "and I'll check on the plane. If the Lord wants you to go, there'll be an empty seat." He did, and we went. It turned out to be golden moments of fellowship and enjoyment.

The public often has a distorted view of older people. A recent survey indicates that 51 percent of the general public look on the elderly as having poor health, while only 20 percent of folk over 65 feel they have health problems. Sixty percent of the population think of older people as lonely, while only 12 percent of the elderly saw themselves as actually lonely. Over 60 percent of those surveyed thought of older people's income as too low to live on, but only 16 percent of the aged had that feeling. About 50 percent thought the elderly were threatened by crime, but only 25 percent of the golden-agers felt thus endangered.

A Christian's attitude and his outlook are the keys to his continuing youth. The grumpy ones will probably age early. The joyful ones, with a song on their lips, seem to stay young forever.

One of the most enjoyable men we know is Dr. Carlton Booth, who for many years led the singing at Keswick and other summer conferences. Likewise, at certain times he conducted vast congregations that flocked to hear Billy Graham, Gypsy Smith and other great evangelists. Even though long retired and in his middle seventies, he retains the youthful vigor he had twoscore years ago. He also serves on nearly two dozen mission boards as part of his stewardship commitment. But I suppose one of the things that characterizes him best is the word "spontaneity."

I have attended brittle business meetings where a funny phrase or hilarious line from Dr. Booth broke the tension and turned the conference into a success. Probably the fondest remembrances, however, are those little personal notes that he jots regularly to his many friends. One of them came to me at a particularly nerve-racking time:

"Dear Ed, Remember, you don't have to pace the deck when the Captain is at the helm!"

A few weeks ago I saw a man in his eighties demonstrate his skills in self-defense. "I'll never retire," he said. "I'm having too much fun." During World War I, Bill Underwood taught doughboys his style of personal combat which he terms "Defenso." During World War II, the Korean and Vietnam wars, he continued to train GI's in his simple five-step system. Today in his eighties he still appears on television, while also teaching private classes of young (and older) women in street defense against robbery and rape. And all of this he does with a droll humor that makes him appear half his age.

4. *Stay supple*

This may sound impossible to an older person with arthritis or other debilitating diseases. But listen to the story of Pablo Casals as witnessed by Norman Cousins. Cousins met Casals first at his home in Puerto Rico and discovered that the eighty-five-year-old man had a regular routine. Although he had many infirmities, he rose above them. He evidently suffered greatly from rheumatoid arthritis. When he first came into the room to meet Cousins, he was bent over and was breathing heavily with emphysema. His fingers and hands were swollen and clenched tightly.

But when Pablo Casals shuffled to the piano a miracle took place. His fingers seemed to unlock and spread over the keys as he began to play from the "Well-Tempered Clavichord." It was evident that he played the piano almost as well as he did his beloved cello. And as was his lifelong habit, he hummed during his performance without wheezing!

His whole body, said Cousins, seemed transfigured by his music. He was no longer rigid with arthritis. And when he stood he was now erect and alert. Gone was the shuffle and he approached the breakfast table with gusto, took a generous helping and then an invigorating walk along the beach. The love of his life—Bach—had rejuvenated him. Cousins had witnessed a goal-centered miracle—a man restored to youth, an illustration of the Psalm, "who satisfies you with good as long as you live, so that your youth is renewed like the eagle's" (Ps. 103:5, RSV).

We probably need to make a clear distinction between growing old and growing stale. Some Christians seem to have "staled out" in their 40s or 50s—or even younger. Others with true spontaneity have reached their 70s, 80s or 90s without achieving the stereotypes of "old age." It is the individual who must set his own pattern. If he is mentally and physically alert, if he thinks young and refuses to live in the past, he can move forward with vigor.

Some twenty-five years ago, I attended graduate school at Temple University's School of Theology where many of the seminars were taught by Dr. Andrew Blackwood. A graduate of Harvard and Princeton, he had been for twenty years the professor of Homiletics at Princeton's School of Divinity. When I studied under him, he was seventy-four years old and still spry. Many of his twenty-five helpful books were published during this latter period of his life.

One of the traits that endeared Andrew Blackwood to his students was his flexible outlook. One day I asked him if he ever planned to retire and he replied, "Never! I don't plan ever to sit under an orange tree in Florida and rust to death."

Interestingly, Dr. Blackwood's greatest work, *The Fine Art of Preaching*, was not published until he was fifty-five. And one of his most helpful volumes, *Expository Preaching for Today*, was published in his seventy-second year. I can still hear his eloquence when he became enthused, even in his latter years, over the subject of preaching for his Lord.

But so many people give up too soon. "Most people," said comedian George Burns recently, "are in rehearsal for old age from the time they're twenty-five or thirty. They are already planning their retirement at forty. It's hard to learn to be old. So folks start learning to walk slowly and forget things and get absent-minded and foggy. Well, by the time they're sixty, sixty-five, they're getting real good at being old, so that when they're seventy, hallelujah—now they're old."

But in order to maintain youth even in advanced years, we must remain continually active, the subject of the following pages.

1 / Keep Active

Dr. Oswald Hoffman, of the Lutheran Hour, recently said in a sermon: "I had a friend of seventy-five who never got old. He was always young, with young ideas, young ways of doing things, a youthful approach to all of life, always getting ready for tomorrow and looking forward with excitement to the day after tomorrow." When asked about his attitude on aging, this same friend said, "All the sugar is at the bottom of the cup!"

The ability to take pleasure in constructive activity helps the older person to cope successfully with life changes. It is a strategic adapting technique that is often omitted from discussion of the "tasks of aging." In looking at our life changes during aging, the ability to take pleasure in our activities is a primary growth need toward continuing maturity. As soon as we accept the importance of pleasurable activity we find ourselves dealing not only with the *problem* of aging, but also with its opportunities.

The Christian who has a pleasant involvement with his present will not need to reminisce about old times and cling to memories. If a person is aging successfully, we can infer that he has the ability to replace his old losses with new and successful ventures.

When I was a lad I had a pastor named Harris Gregg who was then in his mid-seventies. By the time our church called him, he had long since attained national attention for his excellent Bible training. Our pastorate was probably a "retirement" vocation for him, although he worked hard as our spiritual shepherd.

Our young people visited his parsonage regularly, for he seemed so young in his outlook. His alert mind and busy schedule belied his years. He encouraged each of us and gave us some guidance from which I have always profited:
- Keep reading widely.
- Keep interested in people and things.

- Keeping thinking constructively.
- Keep studying the Word.

Some of the following are actions we need to hold in focus as we follow through on these basic concepts:

1. *Keep adjusting physically and socially*

Making allowance for our advancing years and slowing bodies is one of the graces we can acquire.

Patricia Leimbach, writing in *Woman's Day*, gives some humorous insight into the dilemmas of growing maturity in a column entitled, "Life at Midstream":

"Middle age," she remarks, "is when you find out where the action is so you can go someplace else."

Concerning our declining strength she says, "Middle age is when you no longer pull out the stove when you paint the kitchen."

And regarding our physique, she remarks, "Middle age is when your age and your hipline begin to approximate each other."

Dr. Ray Ortlund and his wife Anne (in their book *The Best Half of Your Life*) tell about the ninety-eight-year-old "Aunt Nancy" who kept active, but had to make adjustments for her physical limitations. She lived in a nursing home and was bedridden. One day a friend brought her an African violet in full bloom. Soon she began to root some of its leaves in other pots which in their turn also blossomed.

One day a visitor saw Aunt Nancy's room all aglow with violets and bought one of them. Then more and more were sold as the word spread, until she had accumulated a fairly good sum. In time, this aged servant of God was able to partially support a missionary in India.

There is little reason why with flexibility, imagination and dedication any of us cannot keep active in his or her own way. Age is no longer a barrier and horizons are now unlimited.

One man grappled with his retirement problems—the adjustment needed, the sudden halt to accustomed activities being difficult hurdles for him at first. Just after he decided to retire, he felt a sense of release and ecstasy. He did not waken any longer with tension, a tight chest or clenched fists, but felt free to lie in bed for a bit. No longer did he get midnight phone calls from upset clients or angry bosses. He was his own man.

But then a reaction set in. After a few months he began to have a let-down feeling and was depressed and shaky. He had formerly spent much of his time attending seminars, researching books, consulting experts and planning schedules. For years he had been grooming himself along a planned career path. But now this had been obliterated by the simple act of retirement. The old daily schedules were no longer required and he felt lost.

Slowly he began to acquire new routines and priorities. He had to rebuild his world, using old skills in new settings with new goals. His activity, after a time of self-assessment, was on the road to a revised and exciting new life structure.

A recent study in Kansas City surveyed the efficacy of what it termed "disengagement." It was the theory that when people retired, they disassociated themselves from society into a kind of social limbo. However, the study also indicated much evidence to the contrary—namely, that not even *very old* people need become totally disengaged. Those between 70 and 74 apparently still had a large number of roles in society. Over 30 percent had a high degree of daily interactions with others. Nearly 20 percent enjoyed "large life space" (i.e., good social life) and another 20 percent did not view their social life as restricted.

A longitudinal survey found that the long-term socializers simply did not make good "disengagers" and were unable to achieve "internal rigidity." In other words, most older people continued to mix as well as they had in earlier years. A three-nation study (in the U.S., Great Britain and Denmark) confirmed that the majority of older people continued to engage themselves in a successful manner.

2. *Keep alert*

Lou Cottin lives in New York City and regards himself a champion of the nation's senior citizens—an advocate of the 25 million people in the United States who are over sixty-five. As he says, "You don't become a non-person or a non-contributor just because you retire."

Because of his alertness, he now writes a column called "Growing Older" that appears in 475 newspapers. He has also, with his wife Nikka, just published a book called *Elders in Rebellion, a Guide to Senior Activities*. Through this he says, "We are fighting for some positive changes."

When he and Nikka had entered their sixties, they decided they needed to think through this whole matter of retirement. Lou spent three hours a day in the library of the National Council on Aging and has now built up his own library of over one hundred books on the subject.

In 1973, *Newsday* on Long Island asked him to write about his old-age advocacy. This was the beginning of his nationwide column.

"We elders," he says, "deserve no special consideration unless we earn it by what we do for ourselves and others. See what you can do for others. Don't sit around and wait for someone to do something for you or come to see you.

"Join the 3.5 million elder volunteers who already are sharing their abilities, expertise, time and love with children, the handicapped or other senior citizens. Volunteer to work for politicians, schools, neighborhood centers or charitable institutions."

Lou strongly promotes multipurpose senior centers which offer lectures, workshops, recreational programs and social events. Most of all he urges senior citizens to expand their minds by reading and enrolling in school programs. And he quotes with approval from Judge Harold Medina who is now ninety-one: "When you use your mind, you make a perceptible impact on your well-being! Older people must restore their status in being useful, interesting people who are nice to be with."

As we observe some older Christians we realize that there are some giants among us who live through much of their lives with great dignity. But sadly, there are also mean and disagreeable older Christian folk. They do not reach into the inner core of their redeemed self but cling to childhood concepts that power and privilege are the only indices of human worth."

The Mexicans have a folk saying akin to this thought. "El

hombre vale por lo que es, no por lo que tiene."—A man is valued by what he is, not by what he has!

3. *Keep interested and interesting*

In her biography of Woodrow Wilson, Ruth Cranston includes this passage on one of the secrets of that leader's great charisma: "Woodrow Wilson's classes were the most popular in the history of Princeton University, and they were far from being snap courses. Year after year the students voted Wilson their most popular teacher." Said one scholar, "He was the most inspiring teacher I have ever sat under." Another commented, "There was about him an aliveness that was infectious."

Whatever the subject, the interested person flows with enthusiasm that lends a halo to a topic or even to a saleable product. What a Christian sees in the things and people around him is probably what others will see in him. If he sees God's world as a bright, lovely and exciting place, his friends will see him as interesting and lively. But if he looks on life as a boring show, he will seem unimaginative and boring. A vital will to live lends enthusiasm to each day—and not just a dull desire to survive. Anyone who takes an infectious interest in things about him will seem far younger than his years.

One man at the age of eighty-five exemplifies this beautifully. His neighbors call him the "grandpa of gourds." Living in the sun belt, he puts pleasure before business. He often sits down before his pile of saleable gourds and strums his ukelele. "Bubbles," he sings in a lively voice, "tiny bubbles . . . " Then after he finishes that song, he modulates into another, "Oh, the old gourd king, he ain't what he used to be . . ."

"His dress is as lively as his spirit," says the *Los Angeles Times*. Wearing a Hawaiian shirt and orange paint-speckled pants, he brightens up his storage lot.

He is a broker of gourds, buying them from growers and selling at a small margin to gourd merchandisers. Whenever he begins to make too much money, he trims his prices. He sells thousands, for instance, to Hawaiian buyers who turn the gourds into native drums for the islands. "We sell them," he reports, "for about one dollar. When they get them to Hawaii, they often sell them for $20 to handicrafters."

Others buy them to make into bird houses, planters and ornaments. This lively man himself creates many of these objects, painting and varnishing them for holiday souvenirs.

Until 1956 he had been a scientist, but when he retired to a cottage on a two-acre lot, his family suggested he try growing gourds. He did cultivate them for a while, but eventually gave most of that up in favor of a middle-man's job. He still grows a few vines, even making his own fertilizer from rotted vegetation. "Anything that smells that bad," he says, "has got to be good fertilizer!"

Today he stores as many as 100,000 gourds in his front and back yards, putting them into neatly-sized piles. "Not one of them is ugly," he insists, "and I love this work. When you work with people and nature, you're not deteriorating." Here is a person who is an interested and happy man—and an interesting one.

A panel of geriatric experts (authorities on the diseases of old age) recently revealed the importance of staying actively interested in things. Those who allow themselves to vegetate may display depression, apathy, irritability, memory loss and unrealistic thinking. Intelligence, according to medical studies, remains stable throughout life with some minor decline after seventy. But degeneration in mental and physical ability usually stems from inactivity. It has been observed that four out of every hundred people over sixty are physically and mentally incapable of social interaction. But this happily implies that ninety-six percent are capable of a great deal of interaction. It simply depends on one's outlook and uplook.

Albert Schweitzer, the medical missionary, remained actively involved in his ministry until his early nineties. He made daily rounds in his Lambarane Hospital almost until the day of his death. At eighty-seven he physically assisted in building a half-mile of road near his compound. And after it was finished, he designed and helped build a stone bridge.

4. *Keep your daring*

It is inspiring to see how many active older people are attempting things that seem "far out" for their age.

Louise Dingwall, for instance, a young grandmother of seventy-nine, had trained many racehorses in her day when she decided to attempt racing for herself. In 1976, her eighty-second year, she rode two horses to victory at the English National Hunt season.

In a study at Duke University, it was learned that individuals such as Louise, who were over sixty-five and who came for regular medical checkups, showed no physical deterioration. This was especially true when they had a record of continued bodily exercise. Indeed, the evidence indicated that a goodly number showed improvement as they continued their daily regimen. Most people can develop a pattern of coping known as an "aging adapter" when they faithfully pursue their personal schedule. This survival device involves each person's unique and God-given ability to do these things:

a. Sense the sum total of one's problem in the aging process.

b. Generate the drive to find a way out.

c. Create a solution to the situation that entraps one.

Florence Bell, a motorcyclist from England, was seventy-seven when her insurance company refused to renew her coverage. She had been accustomed to riding an easy two hundred miles regularly. When she tried to get another policy from a different agency, they too refused. She kept searching until finally one broker, hearing of her predicament, discovered that she had an accident-free record and found a company that would insure her.

Obviously, riding racehorses or motorcycles are two ventures that most of us might not choose. But there are still the many overseas trips, the unusual hikes, the daily side trips that can add zest to living. Small business ventures, the hobbies of painting or bricklaying, or a thousand-and-one other things can flavor a life. Costs on many of these are minimal—or indeed nothing at all—if one shops around.

I have a sister-in-law who has limited means but in her sixties arranges trips every year to Europe or Latin America. Dot searches out the lowest excursion rates, contacts missionary friends with whom she can stay, and enjoys high adventure. Her bright friendliness opens many doors and she has toured Italy,

England, and Canada among other places.

Last year she visited a missionary friend in Bolivia just at the time of the revolution. "I wouldn't have chosen it in advance, if I had known," she told me, "but I wouldn't have missed it for the world!" The Lord protected her and she came back to give inspiring mission talks in New England churches.

There is a need for adventure in the heart of the Christian, and the majority of broken lives are probably suffering because this need has been repressed and is eating away at one's insides. (The Gospel itself is the springboard for the world's most exciting adventure!) For many people, their upbringing, their failures, their social responsibility—all seem to have *overwhelmed* their adventurous nature which should have been continually encouraged to expand and to indulge in what Tournier calls "spontaneous fantasy."

5. *Keep studying*

"Stretch your mind!" Dr. Culbert Rutenber used to tell his students at Eastern Baptist Seminary. "Don't just read the funnies or the sports page. Let your mind grow until you die."

Scientific research has now disproved this ancient belief: "Your mind deteriorates as you grow older!" The brain cells in the human mind are lost at only 100 thousand per day, while 20 *billion* brain cells remain—a loss one can readily afford. At this attrition rate, it would take hundreds of years to lose them all.

Many older folk are now returning to school. They are getting acquainted with Aristotle, German grammar or embroidery. One ninety-year-old is brushing up on her French so that she can attend the Sorbonne in Paris. Another group in a retirement home is using flash cards to learn eighteenth-century European history.

IBM is now offering $2500 each to its retirees so that they and their spouses can take continuing education in the years following retirement. At present 1.7 million Americans over fifty-five are taking courses in higher education.

Increasingly aware of this previously untapped source of students, nearly twenty percent of U.S. colleges are offering courses slanted toward the older population. Among state colleges and universities, almost half give free tuition to older citizens, according to Ruth Weinstock in her book, *The Greying of the Campus*.

Unfortunately, some of the courses can be termed "golden-age garbage," such as belly-dancing, kazoo-playing and astrology. But many worthwhile courses are satisfying the felt needs of older people. These strivings can be divided into four categories:

1. *Coping needs*: Economic or social self-sufficiency needs can be met by cooking, finances, legal skills or even "living alone and liking it." Christians can find some of these needs met in larger churches, YMCA's, as well as Christian colleges.

2. *Expressive needs*: Talents that have lain dormant for many years and can now be expressed in courses like handcrafts, music, writing and the arts.

3. *Intellectual needs*: Long-felt yearnings for a better understanding of our culture through literature, music, history or language can be satisfied in college courses. Here, too, is a long-neglected opportunity for deeper Bible study.

4. *Activist needs*: The desires to feel needed, to raise funds for missions, to exert wholesome political influence, and the like must be channeled.

The Miami-Dade Community College now offers courses to nearly four thousand senior people. The project director reports, "They come in here like eighteen-year-olds right out of high school. They just want to learn!" These older students often feel out-of-place, asking, "Will I fit in with all these young people?" And professors quickly reply, "Yes, because school is for the young in thought."

One bit of preparation teachers advocate for these seniors is that they take refreshers in study skills, perhaps through reading from the library stacks or from recent newspapers, magazines and periodicals. Attending a few weekend courses at senior centers or private schools also helps. Twenty states now offer short-term refresher programs such as the week-long summer refreshers at Arizona State University—termed Elder Hostels. Information can be obtained by writing to 55 Chapel Street, Newton, Maine 02160. For further help, one can also write the Institute of Lifetime Learning, 1909 K Street, Washington, D.C. 20049.

Christians can go on educating themselves throughout their lives. An important factor in remaining young is the longing to learn and understand. The willingness to initiate something, to attempt and to persevere, to correct one's errors, to push for improvement, to experience new things, to constantly gain proficiency, to widen one's horizons and to stand on one's tiptoes in expectancy—these things are vital for an active older "youth."

It is to seek such new paths of learning and endeavor that one turns to the gift of creativity, the subject we will next examine.

CHECKLIST FOR YOUR RETIREMENT ACTIVITIES

1. Skills and qualifications you have (check one or more):

   Teaching ability _____
   Handcraft skills _____
   Writing ability _____
   Secretarial or typing skills _____
   Photographic ability _____
   Childcare skills _____
   Gifts in helping people _____
   Language abilities _____
   Cooking skills _____
   Helping the handicapped _____
   Medical know-how _____
   Public speaking ability _____
   Skills with older people _____
   Library knowledge _____
   Sales ability _____
   Love of church work _____
   Artistic skills _____
   Musical gifts _____
   Other abilities _____
   _____
   _____
   _____
   _____

2. Next, assess the activities you have liked and would want to pursue in later years:

List the jobs and other activities that have given you happiness in your life:	Most	Somewhat	Least
_____	_____	_____	_____
_____	_____	_____	_____
_____	_____	_____	_____
_____	_____	_____	_____
_____	_____	_____	_____
_____	_____	_____	_____

3. List unusual skills and
   abilities you have
   displayed: Best   Moderate   Least

	Best	Moderate	Least
_____	_____	_____	_____
_____	_____	_____	_____
_____	_____	_____	_____
_____	_____	_____	_____
_____	_____	_____	_____

4. *Now try to remember those
   things you liked* about the
   performance of your jobs:

	Much	Some	Little
Applying yourself to your job or profession	_____	_____	_____
Achieving something useful	_____	_____	_____
Serving the Lord	_____	_____	_____
Helping others	_____	_____	_____
Achieving status	_____	_____	_____
Receiving appreciation	_____	_____	_____
Feeling needed	_____	_____	_____
Solving problems	_____	_____	_____
Doing routine tasks	_____	_____	_____
Receiving reward or pay	_____	_____	_____

5. Next ask yourself about *your
   personal characteristics*.
   Do you:

	Much	Some	Little
Want to accomplish things?	_____	_____	_____
Work out your own ideas?	_____	_____	_____
Prefer to be alone?	_____	_____	_____
Like to lead others?	_____	_____	_____
Get easily bored?	_____	_____	_____
Read a great deal?	_____	_____	_____
Watch a lot of TV?	_____	_____	_____
Enjoy outdoor work?	_____	_____	_____
Take regular exercise?	_____	_____	_____
Feel guilty about unfinished tasks?	_____	_____	_____

Have a lot of friends?   _____ _____ _____
Like to work with congenial
    folks?   _____ _____ _____
Have many hobbies?   _____ _____ _____
Have to be punctual?   _____ _____ _____
Go out a lot?   _____ _____ _____
Have much interest
    in sports?   _____ _____ _____
Stick to the job until it's
    finished?   _____ _____ _____
Like to have recognition for
    your work?   _____ _____ _____

6. Finally, using the information from the above lists,
   place in order of priority
   the activities you might
   *most likely want to follow
   in your retirement*:   Most   Some   Least

   a. _____   _____ _____ _____
   b. _____   _____ _____ _____
   c. _____   _____ _____ _____
   d. _____   _____ _____ _____
   e. _____   _____ _____ _____
   f. _____   _____ _____ _____
   g. _____   _____ _____ _____

2 / Keep Creative

Anna Mary Robertson was 76 years old when she stopped stitching and started painting. After embroidering for 50 years, arthritis stiffened the joints of her hands. After meditating on her impasse for a while she decided to try painting as her next vocation. In the next 25 years she painted 250 of the finest "primitives" of this century. Even in her final year of life, Grandma Moses painted 20 colorful masterpieces—at the age of 101!

"When I was seventy-six," she recalled, "my fingers were hurting so much that I had to stop embroidering. Suddenly I thought: 'Why not try painting?' I knew about colors and composition from my embroidery. It seemed like a natural transition!"

Rollo May calls such creative revelation "the fourth stage of consciousness—a burst of enlightenment that pops into the mind almost unbidden." It was this same sudden awareness that Helen Keller experienced when from her darkened world she spoke her first word, "Water!"

In these instances the person has wrestled over a period of time for an answer to a problem or puzzle. All at once, and seemingly from nowhere, comes the answer for which he has been struggling.

Such insight may involve the attempt to implement new life-vision, using the most appropriate tools available. Our fifties and sixties are a time of searching for a new role, perhaps a new relationship—and maybe of forming fresh surroundings suitable to these goals. Sometimes a checklist is helpful in choosing an avocation, a hobby, at this time:

	Yes	Somewhat	No
1. Is what I am planning to do agreeable with my physical ability?		✓	

2. Does it agree with my
   lifestyle interests?   _____✓ _____ _____

3. Do I have the facilities to
   pursue this interest?   _____✓ _____ _____

4. Can I afford it?   _____✓ _____ _____

5. Can I possibly make some
   money with it?   _____ _____ _____✓

6. Can I get some additional
   benefit—such as socializing?   _____ _____ _____✓

7. Does it glorify God and is it
   consistent with my Christian
   faith?   _____ _____✓ _____

If you find that you can answer "yes" or "somewhat" to all of these questions, you are probably nearing the right choice.

At times our vision may take the form of a dream like that of Elias Howe who envisioned the proper needle for his new invention and created the machine that altered the clothing world, the modern sewing machine. In other instances, a time of spiritual meditation may provide the answer, even in cases when one may not be concentrating on the problem.

My son-in-law unravels difficulties somewhat in this fashion when working on his car. Rather than work fruitlessly, he occupies himself with another project, or perhaps takes a nap. When he awakes and returns to the car, his mind, working unconsciously, has given him the answer.

This process we popularly refer to as "comes the dawn!" Gestalt psychologists call it the "aha!" experience—when the mind puts all the puzzle pieces together.

1. Insight

Recently I visited Taliesin West where Frank Lloyd Wright established an architectural school at age sixty-five. There I saw many brilliant examples of his creative genius.

In his autobiography, Wright tells about his preacher father and teacher mother who early taught him to look for form and meaning within natural structures. "Taken East at the age of three," he relates, "to my father's pastorate near Boston . . . I remember sitting at the little kindergarten table and playing upon 'unit lines' with cubes and spheres and tripods." It was an early "dawn experience" for young Frank. "The virtue in all this," he continues, "lay in the awakening of my child mind to rhythmic structures in nature."

In Sunday school, the verse making the greatest impression on Frank's formative mind was Matthew 6:28. Sixty years later he said, "Simplicity is a reward for fine feeling and straight thinking. . . . Solomon knew nothing about it, for he was only wise. And this, I think, is what Jesus meant by the text . . . 'Consider the lilies of the field' as contrasted for beauty with Solomon." This thought worked subconsciously in Wright for eighty years, giving birth to numerous insights for his world-famous organic architecture.

At age eighty, having studied the giant saguaro cactus with its fine proportion and natural ribbing, he designed his mile-high skyscraper. No one has yet had the courage to build this graceful structure, but 500 other buildings around the world attest to his creativity.

"The skeleton rudiment, accepted and understood, is the first condition of any fruit or flower we may hope to get for ourselves," he said of his basic structural concept.

At age sixty-nine, Wright conceived the idea of "Falling Water," a captivating house in Bear Run, Pennsylvania. And at age ninety-three, the last year of his life, he completed two of his masterpieces. One was the Guggenheim Museum on Fifth Avenue in New York. The interior of this is dominated by a spiral ramp running upward from the bottom floor to the top—possibly a symbol of man's rising artistic aspirations. The other building, to be completed in the 1990s, is the Marin County (CA) Civic Center, a reflection of the eternal hills surrounding San Francisco.

His principle of organic simplicity was well expressed in his words spoken during his sixty-fifth year: "Five lines, where three are enough, is stupidity. Nine pounds where three are sufficient is also stupidity."

Creative awareness like Wright's or Grandma Moses' approaches a state of "ecstasy"—a Greek derivative meaning to "stand outside oneself"—or a person going beyond himself.

The Bible tells us the same secret: We must first lose our life in dedication before we can find ourselves in achievement (Mark 8:35; John 12:24, 25).

2. *Self-expression*

The center of our difficulty often is that our problem is an inner, not an outer one. We must look within and set personal goals first. There is no happiness in a goal-less existence and we cannot feel fulfilled when life has no meaning. The goal we Christians choose may often seem silly or meaningless to another, but will remain deeply significant to us. Our goal must match our person, and will probably remain with us until death.

One of the most interesting men in pursuit of a personal goal is Eiffel Plasterer—known as "Mr. Bubbles." He is eighty years old but seems eternally young as he studies the structure of the common bubble. He was a science teacher, but eventually abandoned this profession to examine the molecular structure of soap film.

Many times a year, according to Jerry Miller in the *American Journal*, he presents what he terms his "Bubble Concerto." He has given more than 1200 performances of this to audiences large and small—to Rotarians, church groups and school assemblies.

From his youth, soap bubbles have fascinated him. He has created long-lasting bubbles, square bubbles, bubbles-inside-bubbles, and bubbles that erupt into flames.

His first public presentation in a PTA meeting has led to even greater things. His largest bubble measured twenty-seven inches across. His oldest bubble lasted 259 days (sealed in a bottle), recorded by Robert Ripley.

But the most beautiful part of Eiffel's story is that it expresses the inner searching of his soul. He views the bubble as a type, or symbol, of personal creation, similar (but on a vastly lower level) to the earth God created.

"It says," Eiffel cites Scripture, "when the Lord created the world, it was without form." He makes an imaginary globe with his hands and says: "Thus when we take a solution of soap, it has no form of its own."

Then with a crescendo, he orates, "By our own breath we blow a bubble that does have form. We're paralleling the creation of the world itself."

Clearly, it is Mr. Plasterer's sense of creativity which makes him amazingly durable. Those who lose this progenerative life-wish are not long for this world. Involvement and viable goals are essential—not merely possessing a blind desire for survival. When we look around we often see elderly Christians who do take such a lively interest in their vocation or hobby and in their world, and they seem far younger than their years.

A person reveals his real self by the way he rises above what people expect from him, and chooses his very personal type of self-expression. "Each person," says Tournier, "plays the card he holds, and that is his adventure."

One denies one's self as a person unless he or she makes creative use of inborn or lifelong talents. Anyone who tries to avoid the inner urging arouses in himself a sense of guilt. And in the last analysis, a person can ruin his or her life by neglecting this God-given drive. "So stir up the gift that is in you," says the Apostle Paul.

3. Overcoming handicaps

Merely because one has grown old, crippled or handicapped is not excuse enough for neglecting his inner call. A person who rises above his difficulty stays young forever.

In 1945, General Douglas MacArthur stated his philosophy, "You don't get old from living a particular number of years: you get old because you have deserted your ideals. Years wrinkle your skin; renouncing your ideals wrinkles your soul. Worry, doubt, fear and despair are the enemies which slowly bring us down to the ground and turn us to dust before we die."

Webster's Dictionary defines courage as "that quality of mind which enables one to encounter difficulties with valor." Ernest Hemingway called it "grace under pressure."

A remarkable parade of courageous handicapped people marches through history. The lad Klaus Spahni of Spain painted countless landscapes, though his arms and legs were hopelessly paralyzed. Klaus painted with a brush in his teeth. Pieter Molevold of Holland, an artist confined to an iron lung in his final years, learned to paint just as skillfully with a brush between his toes. He reproduced his former paintings so flawlessly that experts could not distinguish his earlier hand-painted work from the foot-painted landscapes of his so-called "old age."

Ealon Lamphier, an auto mechanic from Stowe, Ohio, was crippled by polio in 1949. In 1954 he started experimenting with mouth-painting, and by 1975 art critics were giving his landscapes rave reviews. Lamphier is also a short-wave enthusiast and describes his life philosophy succinctly: "Life is what you make it. Each of us must overcome some handicap—either a physical disability, limited education, insufficient money, or simply lack of confidence. I have gained not only an income, but the inspiration to live creatively."

Likewise, Viola Hamby of Vancouver, Washington, tells how art has helped her to enjoy her life fully. She was born with nerve and muscle damage to her arms but learned to paint with a brush between her teeth. "Painting," she says, "is a way for me to experience things vicariously. When I was a child I couldn't roller skate. So I drew a picture of a little girl on skates. What I couldn't do, I drew. Pretty soon I found that art helped in lots of ways. Nowadays I'm really living life to the hilt."

A psychiatrist recently received a letter from a patient, who said, "It is much easier to be in the position of a victim than in that of a person conscious of his responsibilities and the gifts he is endowed with. But the latter person has found the only way to inner maturity. How difficult it is really to accept one's life as it is and be creative within one's limitations. But I know that everything comes back to that creative acceptance—and *that is the real key to one's happiness.*"

4. *Using spiritual strength*

A recent survey of successful and mature men and women showed that a vast majority attributed their achievements to God's indwelling power in one way or another. And this extended to the small tasks of life as well:

"Since I have been sweeping my floors with God," said an elderly housekeeper, "I have the strength to do more and do it better."

Paul Tournier always asked himself: "Is my little personal adventure in harmony with the great adventure of God?"

Jomo Kenyatta, one of the greatest recent black leaders of Africa, was uncertain of where or when he was born. "I do not know," he said, "when I was born, what date, what month, or what year." His birth was probably near Nairobi around 1890. But he was early instilled with the teachings of Christ through missionaries of the Church of Scotland. A love of country and a hatred of oppression were by-products of his education.

Jailed for his beliefs, he fought constantly for Kenya's national independence, and at the age of about seventy-three, he became its first prime minister. His first words to his former English opponents at the time of truce were a reflection of deep Christian beliefs: "I forgive you; do you forgive me?"

During the next fifteen years, although surrounded by corruption, he kept an abiding awareness of God's presence, and performed a miracle of unity for his country. Drawing together the nation's diverse population of Africans, Arabs, Asians and Europeans, he became one of the first African leaders to establish a working, peaceful coalition government on that continent.

God's strength within is the secret of life's success, but lack of it results in personal disintegration. Edna St. Vincent Millay described this in her 1912 poem, "Renascence," which reflected her spiritual commitment at the age of nineteen:

> The world stands out on either side
> No wider than the heart is wide
> Above the world is stretched the sky,
> No higher than the soul is high.
> The soul can push the sea and land
> Farther away on either hand;

The soul can split the sky in two,
And let the face of God shine through—
But east and west will pinch the heart
That cannot keep them pushed apart;
And he whose soul is flat—the sky
Will cave in on him by and by.

5. *And living deeper*

The Lord reminds us: "Out of [the heart] are the issues of life" (Prov. 4:23, KJV), creatively flowing and releasing us to new possibilities. To become rigid, dogmatic and unmoved by wonder is to stifle the heart. The wholeness of Christian action derives from harmony with one's inward motives.

"Blessed are the pure in heart," Jesus told His disciples, "for they shall see God" (Matt. 5:8, KJV). The twice-born person looks within at reflections of the indwelling Lord and creatively interprets this vision with his hands. Sometimes it is a painting, sometimes a statue, or perhaps another creation, but only as beautiful as it is true to one's reborn self.

Listening to this deepest self enabled George Washington Carver to fill his days and the whole world with the wealth of his creativity. In 1940, his eightieth year, Carver related the secret of his discovering many uses for the lowly peanut: "The thing that I am to do and the way of doing it came to me from God. The method is revealed at the moment I am inspired to create something new!" Using all the knowledge accumulated from agricultural scientists as well as his own experiments, he waited for the voice of God. "I love to think of nature as an unlimited broadcasting system," he often told his students at Tuskegee, "through which God speaks to us every hour, if only we will tune Him in."

By the time of his death at eighty-five, Carver had created a total of three hundred products derived from the peanut. Their range staggers the mind: mayonnaise, instant coffee, cheese, chili sauce, bleach, axle grease, metal polish, adhesives, wood stains, linoleum, plastics and wallboard, to name only a few. With the simple peanut, Carver proved that man could provide almost everything he needed. Today, over 1,000 scientists at the Agricultural Department perform follow-up on the work that George Carver—with God—pioneered.

The integrating principle for this brilliant but humble man was found in a ragged Bible given him by Aunt Mariah Watkins when he was converted in a Methodist church at the age of twelve. Great portions of Genesis, the Psalms, Proverbs and the Gospels remained deep in his heart throughout his life.

In 1938, when asked by 1,000 students at MacAlester College how he chose the peanut, seventy-five-year-old Carver told them a parable. "When I was young, I asked the Lord, 'Dear Mr. Creator, tell me what man was made for?' He answered me, 'Little man, you are asking for more than you can handle. Cut down your request and improve your intent!' So then I asked, 'Lord, why did You make the peanut?' 'That's better,' He said, and He gave me a handful of peanuts and went with me to the laboratory and together we got down to work!"

In all his eighty-five years, Carver never let one day pass without spending at least an hour with God. He lived from deep within himself and beheld inner visions.

6. *And deeper*

The greater a person's awareness of himself and God, the more he can acquire wisdom from the universe in order to create meaningful work. Meister Eckhardt, the medieval Christian, said, "No one has known God who has not known himself—so fly to your soul which is the secret place of the Most High!"

Each day presents new opportunity and excitement—and each of us stands on the threshold of a shining new room. Perceiving this, Oliver Wendell Holmes, when he was fifty, began exploring what he termed the "underground workshop of thought." Among his interesting poems pursuing this theme is his poem, *The Chambered Nautilus*, a study of the exotic shellfish as a parable of life. Just as the nautilus moves from smaller to larger chambers in his shell, walling himself off from past achievements, so we should always be attempting greater things:

Build thee more stately mansions, O my soul,
As the swift seasons roll!
Leave thy low-vaulted past!
Let each new temple, nobler than the last

Shut thee from heaven with a dome more vast
Till thou at last are free
Leaving thine outgrown shell by life's unresting sea!

In order to keep moving ahead, however, we need to keep ourselves from "hardening viewpoints"—ever flexible to explore new horizons. It is with this that we shall next concern ourselves.

CHECKLIST FOR CHOOSING CREATIVE OUTLETS

1. Think back and try to analyze how
   you have created things in the past. **Yes   Some   No**

   a. Have you been *imaginative* in
      finding new ways to do things,
      make up stories, paint pictures,
      etc.?   ___ ___ _✓_

   b. Have you been *inventive* with
      new gadgets, ways of repairing or
      fixing, building, etc.?   ___ ___ _✓_

   c. Did you *like to improvise* or
      experiment with new devices?   ___ ___ _✓_

   d. Have you *tried to improve* or
      adapt methods, devices or
      gadgets for new uses?   ___ ___ _✓_

2. Next, try to analyze ways you have
   used intuition: **Yes   Some   No**

   a. Have you shown foresight in
      predicting results or in plan-
      ning ahead?   _✓_ ___ ___

   b. Do you have insight in ways
      things will work or how people
      will react?   _✓_ ___ ___

   c. Have you ever relied on faith in
      decision-making, trusting some-
      one, or stepping into the
      unknown?   ___ ___ _✓_

   d. Can you picture or visualize the
      way something will be from a
      sketch, blueprint or description? ___ ___ _✓_

3. Try to visualize ways you might
   sharpen and enhance your creative
   abilities.

	Yes	Some	No
a. Would a course (or courses) help improve your skill?	✓		
b. Can you discipline yourself for home preparation in this?		✓	
c. Will the costs be in line with your finances?		✓	
d. Is this available locally or by mail?	✓		
e. Have you proven yourself with at least some accomplishment in this field?			✓
f. Do pastors, teachers and others recognize your skills in this?			✓

4. Finally, use this list to check creative
   things that might interest you.

	Much	Some	Little
a. Craft work: bead work, leather work, jewelry, etc.			✓
b. Creative writing: articles, poetry, stories, drama			✓
c. Letter writing, journals, diaries, etc.	✓		
d. Collecting: buttons, bells, rocks, stamps, coins, etc.			✓
e. Acting in plays		✓	
f. Public speaking, teaching, preaching, Bible story telling			✓
g. Art creation, designing, sculpture, painting, pottery, etc.			✓

	Much	Some	Little
h. Culinary arts: baking, cooking, canning, etc.			✓
i. Handiwork, mechanics, carpentry, woodwork			✓
j. Outdoor work: gardening, yard work, farming			✓
k. Decorating: interior design, upholstery, house painting			✓
l. Music: playing an instrument, singing, composing, listening		✓	
m. Handwork: crochet, needlework, knitting, embroidery		✓	
n. Indoor gardening such as houseplants		✓	
o. Refinishing, fixing, or repairing			✓
p. Keeping things neat, house-keeping, homemaking	✓		
q. Service clubs			✓
r. Outdoor life: bird watching, nature study			✓
s. Animal care: horses, dogs, cats			✓
t. Travel interests resulting in photography, slide shows, lectures		✓	
u. Children: day-care-center helper, teacher's aide, playground assistant			✓

3 / Keep Flexible

It was a man of eighty-two who conceived, designed and directed the most daring architectural dome up to his time. Yet he continually protested, "I am not an architect!"

Michaelangelo Buonnarroti had, in effect, been "drafted" to finish St. Peter's Cathedral. In 1557, at age eighty-two, he had constructed in clay a small model of the church's dome. He knew that the width and weight were perils never before hazarded. So in addition, he took an extra year to construct a large wooden model and draw up plans for the cupola's support. He was nearing eighty-five when he conceived a dome 138 feet in diameter, 151 feet high and 334 feet from the ground to the apex. As if this were not daring enough, the aging genius added a smaller cupola 69 feet above the larger one and a giant cross high over all.

When the massive dome finally rose, Michaelangelo left it to younger hands. The titan of art felt that his architectural work was now finished.

But between sixty and ninety, he had built, painted or carved what others would consider a lifetime of beauty. The *Last Judgment* was completed when he was sixty-six. Two of his most beautiful frescoes were done when he was sixty-seven. His Florentine *Pieta* was carved at seventy-five. Yet, surprisingly, he had vainly protested to his patrons as he had at the undertaking in the Sistine Chapel, "This is not my trade. I am only a sculptor!" Michaelangelo, one of the most magnificent painters our world has known, did not consider painting his gift.

Rollo May reminds us: "Freedom means *openness*, a readiness to grow; it means being flexible, ready to change for the sake of greater human values."

As we grow older, we need to think more broadly—not widely—but with clearer vision born of experience and years of learning. Like our Western pioneers, we need to *dare* and to emulate their courage in areas we would perhaps never have tried in our youth.

1. *Taking risks*

In his sixtieth year, Bill Myers lets nothing stand in his way. For thirty years he has cleared every hurdle in his path, always seeking new ways to overcome his obstacles. Yet this man is a quadriplegic due to a progressive form of polio. His doctor had told this wheelchair-bound veteran, "You can do anything you want to try." Bill took him seriously: "I always thought that was the best advice I could have gotten. He gave me no limitations."

Finding the Midwest too difficult in the winter ("My neighbors had to shovel me and my wheelchair out of the snow too often!"), he moved to the sun belt. There, after studying at a state university, he found a job as an architect. But since the use of his arms was limited by paralysis, he "let his fingers do the walking" across the drafting board.

Slowly he perfected the skill of mechanical drawing despite his handicaps. "I have always gone on the theory," he says, "that I have to be better at what I do than my counterparts."

Today he has received citations from many local and national associations for his skills in specification writing. The city's Building Code Committee has also made him a full-fledged member.

He has specialized in building design that will accommodate the handicapped. The city's street curb designs are not approved without his okay.

In his own home, he has solved the problems of narrow doors for the handicapped with his own formulas. His halls, telephone accesses, rooms and light switches meet the needs of the handicapped. He has also designed his wheelchair so that he can go fishing and perform other vigorous activities. Because he flies to other cities to fulfill his duties, he frequently must rent extra batteries for his heavy-duty wheelchair. Now he is attempting to persuade Hertz and Avis to rent twelve-volt batteries for such equipment.

Due to Bill's efforts, many cities are now becoming aware of the needs of wheelchair people. He is presently pressing for a national unified building code that will provide for his handicapped colleagues.

Like this man, we daily discover through risks that there are new opportunities for service as circumstances change in our aging process. Psychiatrist Arthur Fox says, "An aging person should search his mind, his heart and his very bones to find what truly interests him." Every choice we make affects each stage that follows and influences the development of our future personality as well as our success in adapting to our changing world. In order that our self should not stagnate, wise choice is imperative.

2. *Widening perspectives*

Seventy-seven-year-old Frank Ineson is a true example of a man beholding wide horizons. He retired over twenty years ago as an assistant on General MacArthur's staff. Frank served as a missionary in Japan for five additional years and then retired for the second time.

Seeking God's will, he felt a clear call to the poor sections of Hawaii. Not knowing how much money he might need, he and his wife Katherine prayed for guidance and were led to John 21:10, 11 ("Jesus said to them, Bring some of the fish just caught. So Simon Peter went aboard and hauled the net ashore full of large fish, a hundred and fifty-three of them."). Frank and Katherine took this figure as the Lord's answer regarding their monthly money need and prayed for $153. They told no one about it, but made preparations to go; and when they were ready, the first check for $153 arrived. It was not always from the same donor, but exactly $153 was mailed punctually each month for the next several years as Frank and Katherine preached the Gospel in Hawaii. Again seeking the Spirit's call, time came for severance from this work. Frank was now about sixty-five and this was his third retirement.

Next, this Spirit-led couple felt drawn to needy areas around Sao Paulo, Brazil. A great revival was taking place there and they heard the Lord saying, "Go over and help them." For the next several years they shared the Word in the slums and suburbs surrounding that great city. Also collaborating with World Vision's MARC Division, Frank was one of several co-authors of the valuable mission handbook, *Brazil—1980*.

Retirement from the Brazilian effort made this Frank's fourth such departure. But World Vision, seeing a real need for his mission expertise, placed him in charge of its newly-conceived PRAYER CALENDAR. Its outreach steadily grew from zero circulation to over 12,000 prayer partners during the next four years, leading to yet another retirement—his fifth.

Frank and Katherine were not yet ready to stop, despite some serious surgery. God's hand guided them to Worldteam, another missions organization, where they were soon laboring in Haiti's hill-country. Katherine, a registered nurse, shared her nursing skills in the mission hospital, while Frank sought ways for practical Christian witness matching his own talents. His heart was especially touched by the hard-working mothers in rural Haiti who daily walked sixteen miles from their village to purchase food for the family.

Frank's pragmatic mind conceived of a way to fill an obvious need. Financing the venture from his own pocket, he set about establishing a cooperative market in the women's own village. Each morning, using the mission vehicle, Frank drove the sixteen miles and purchased an adequate assortment of vegetables and other foodstuffs, which he delivered to the housewives. Other helpful projects soon followed, and today Frank and Katherine labor there happily for the Lord in their mid-seventies.

Because of his lifelong dedication and support ministry for missionaries, Frank Ineson was given the 1980 "Helping Hands" award by the World Relief Commission of the National Association of Evangelicals.

Professor Havighurst indicates some of the things that usually slow us down as the years advance: "The world no longer seems simple and easy to master just by working at it. Thought begins to replace action as a mode of dealing with the world . . . the body becomes a problem. The decline of physical strength and skill has started in our early fifties and the body is less and less favorable for the operation of the ego."

Nevertheless, the aging person has many choices. "Many

people," he adds, "have the energy and curiosity to create a new lifestyle, one that gives more satisfaction." Wider travel, a new career, new social activities, new hobbies and recreation lie before us as alternatives. It takes only a small amount of courage to step out and try.

3. *Choosing consistently*

To understand our changing selves, psychologists distinguish eight steps in our personality development throughout life. Each of us goes through these eight stages of ego attainment between babyhood and old age. Every time we move to a new step we are confronted by a choice or crisis, and whatever is our decision at each stage may weaken or strengthen all steps that follow. Each choice has its effect on all further choices. Our personality development determines our success or failure in our future world.

When we reach our early sixties we are at the threshold of late adulthood. It is here we decide whether we will become active or become stagnant for the remainder of life.

Erik Erickson uses the term "generativity" to define what he calls "expanding ego interests." In the eighth step of life, the choice is between ego hopefulness and ego despair.

Although crippled by arthritis since 1953, Nellie Sinclair has chosen the hopeful step. Her infectious smile and positive attitude at seventy-five have won her scores of friends. She ignores her pain, and the friends who come to comfort her feel blessed as they leave her nursing home.

Twenty years ago, she established a profitable little gift shop to keep herself busy. Her first products were cat-shaped salt and pepper shakers that mewed when turned over. "I didn't know what to do with them at first," she said, "but then the nurses went crazy over them. The mewing salt and pepper shakers were my first big item."

After that she increased her stock with more variety. She grew plants on her window ledge and sold these as well. Nowadays she is stocking more ceramic items along with cosmetics for her customers—mainly visitors and staff. Through it all, this dear lady maintains a cheery outlook and sense of humor.

"You have to have faith in the Lord," she says. "I enjoy living but I also have God's kingdom to look forward to." She loves to look out the window at God's creation. "I don't have any problems," she smiles. "I think about all the blessings I have—a nice home, nice people, good food—I give thanks for them every day."

Another plus for step eight in life is the freedom it brings from stultifying social mannerisms. As one eighty-year-old put it: "I'm financially independent now, and I've decided I can say what I believe. I've finally found integrity—and I'm enjoying it! I start each day feeling free. Some folks respect me for it and others think I'm senile. But I'm not afraid to say what I think and be my own man."

4. *Facing crises with courage*

Regardless of one's political convictions, most would regard President Harry Truman as a standout crisis-facer. His first crisis was being chosen by F.D.R. as his 1944 running-mate. Notified by the Democratic national chairman Robert Hannigan, he at first refused. "I'm for Jimmy Byrnes," he said. Just then, President Roosevelt called and shouted to Hannigan over the telephone, "Have you got that fellow lined up yet?" "No," said Hannigan, "he is the contrariest Missouri mule I've ever dealt with!" "Well," replied F.D.R., "you tell him that if he wants to break up the Democratic party in the middle of a war, that's his responsibility!" "Now what do you say?" asked Hannigan as he hung up. "Lord, help me," murmured Truman.

In November, he and F.D.R. tasted victory. Truman was then sixty-two.

His next great crisis occurred the day Eleanor Roosevelt called and announced, "Harry, the President is dead!" His first words were, "Is there anything I can do for you?" Her reply: "Is there anything *we* can do for you? You are the one in trouble now!"

After taking the oath of office of President, Truman said to the reporters, "Boys, if you ever pray, pray for me now. I don't know whether you fellows have ever had a load of hay fall on you, but when they told me yesterday what had happened, I felt like the moon, the stars and all the planets had fallen on me!" He was then sixty-three.

His crises piled up: the decision to drop the Bomb in 1945 was one of his hardest; the establishment of the Truman Doctrine to strengthen the allies against Communism in 1946; the declaration of the Marshall Plan in 1947 to rebuild Europe. Above all, the decisions concerning Korea in 1949 and 1950 were filled with crises.

In his spunky campaign of 1948, he ran against highly-favored Thomas Dewey. With his 31,000-mile whistle-stop campaign against a "do-nothing" Congress, he won by two million votes.

As President in his sixties, he arose at 5:30 every day and went for a brisk walk before undertaking heavy duties. He continued to meet Presidential crises with vigor until he was succeeded by Dwight Eisenhower. But life did not end for Truman at sixty-eight when he left the White House. Lectures, books and elder-statesman duties kept him active into his middle eighties. I remember the thrill of having him speak to our graduate classes at New York University when he was seventy-eight—lucid, informed and challenging. By that time he had written two bestsellers: *Years of Decision* (1955) and *Years of Trial and Hope* (1956).

Yet with all his accomplishments, he remained basically humble. In his eighty-seventh year, he refused the Congressional Medal of Honor with the words, "I do not consider that I have done anything which should be the reason for any award, congressional or otherwise."

Others differed with him, however. Winston Churchill said to him on one occasion, "I must confess, sir . . . I loathed your taking the place of Franklin Roosevelt. I misjudged you badly. Since that time, you, more than any other man, have saved Western Civilization."

After his death, Malcolm Muggeridge wrote: "Truman was the last authentic American with all the characteristic faults and virtues of the breed, to occupy the White House, and I doubt very much if there will ever be another."

In Harry Truman at sixty-two we see a person who faced his eighth life-crisis with courage and creativity. Most of his previous life was merely a prelude to his final twenty-five years. He faced the eighth stage with a resounding "yes," and made it one of the most productive the world has ever seen.

Sadly, there are those like Ernest Hemingway who approach the sixty-year threshold with a negative attitude. Hemingway perceived his life as finished and destroyed himself with violence.

Gail Sheehy, in her book *Passages*, says about this step number eight: "The final stage presents the opportunity for *integrity* and might be said to represent the point at which the midlife crisis can be successfully resolved."

Truman in his vice-presidency occupied an office many have considered a dead end. But when greatness was thrust upon him at sixty-two, he grasped it eagerly and made it a life-saver for humanity. Many vice-presidents who succeeded to the presidency did not do so well.

Tournier remarks, "A man changes—why then do so many people think and say the contrary? Perhaps it is an attempt to justify themselves and provide an excuse for not changing." Indeed some say to the world, "What do you expect? This is the way I am made. I cannot change!" Often this is a secret request for someone to say the opposite as reassurance.

"How many disillusioned souls there are who no longer believe that any success is possible in their lives," he concludes. "Success is always possible to a person (yes, even in the last passage of life) who will look, not back, but forward."

A lady from Hollywood recently wrote to the *Los Angeles Times*, "What a lift one of your letters was to me. Just as I was feeling sorry for myself—my husband deceased and the children 'flown the coop'—I began to take stock of myself. I am eighty years old, and even though I am not really in perfect health, I thank God for the things I can still do at my age. I work with blind people, teaching mosaics twice a week, and I still manage a sixteen-unit building. I thank God every day for His strength."

It is out of flexibility such as this lady's that appropriate planning takes place, the subject of the following pages.

Before turning to the next chapter, you may wish to evaluate your personal flexibility with the following questionnaire:

1. A test of your adaptability to new personal
   ventures: Yes   No

   a. Have I done anything in the past 48 hours
      that I could describe as a new venture?   _____ __✓__

      What? _____

   b. Have I recently read a "how to" book or an
      article in any new field?   _____ __✓__

   c. Have I made a new friend within the past
      month? or joined a new group?   _____ __✓__

   d. Have I considered a new idea or
      suggestion in the past week?   _____ __✓__

      What? _____

   e. Have I tried a new food, menu, or recipe
      in the past month?   _____ __✓__

      Name one or more. _____

   f. Have I attempted a new skill, hobby, or
      sport within the past year?   _____ __✓__

   g. Have I tried a new dress or suit fashion in
      the past year?   _____ __✓__

   h. Have I examined my lifestyle recently
      with a view of altering it?   _____ __✓__

   i. Have I sought fresh insight from the Bible
      that might challenge me in new or revived
      service?   _____ __✓__

(A score of 6 or more yesses indicates considerable flexibility on
your part.)

2. Next, try a *depth* analysis of your personal
   flexibility: Yes   No

   a. Do I make an honest attempt to really
      enjoy my new ventures?   _____ _____

b. Am I optimistic about each new venture's
   success? _____ _____

c. Do I relish my successes and try to build
   on them? _____ _____

d. Do I inventory my old habits so that I
   can streamline and make room for
   innovations? _____ _____

e. Am I constantly looking and listening for
   new ideas and techniques? _____ _____

f. Do I seriously set a higher mark to attain
   for the Lord each day? _____ _____

g. Do I participate and listen actively in
   every discussion so that I can learn? _____ _____

h. Do I try to eliminate trivia so that I can
   concentrate on the essential? _____ _____

i. Do I ask myself frequently, "How can I
   best use my time right now?" _____ _____

j. Do I set aside a time each day when I can
   meditate and think creatively about new
   goals? _____ _____

(A score of 6 or more indicates that you have attained a quality of
depth in your flexibility.)

4 / Keep Planning

In my in-laws' family was a Grandfather Harold who, with Irma his wife, reached the age of eighty-five. He always set regular goals for himself. In his final fifteen years, he redesigned and rebuilt his house with *his own hands*. He served as an active member on the board of the community house. He campaigned for the improvement of parks, cemeteries and other neighborhood projects. He and his wife took trips in the spring and fall of each year. Their partnership and their sense of adventure seemed to be the secret of their longevity.

In Eugene O'Neill's play *Ah Wilderness*, he says, "Spring isn't everything. There's a lot to be said for fall and winter, too, if you're together."

And even beyond this sharing, each party in such a union must maintain his or her own personal integrity. Howard Clinebell in *Growth Counseling* comments that "it is crucial that both individuals (in such a couple) continue developing their own inner resources and autonomy."

In planning one's future, the goals one sets for himself should satisfy his needs, should be limited by reality, should fulfill his creative instinct and should be consistent with his real self. Abraham Maslow has conceived a pyramid of needs with a baseline in one's physical requirements but topped off by ego-actualization. In setting one's life-goals it is helpful to keep his hierarchy of needs in mind:

5. Self-actualization
4. Self-esteem
3. Love and Belonging
2. Safety and Security
1. Physical Needs

At the base of his pyramid, or hierarchy, Maslow states the very elemental needs we have for survival. Thus, our food, clothing and shelter should be the focus of our short-range goals.

The second level in his schemata indicates our need for security and self-preservation, with goals geared to personal safety, such as driving defensively, locking doors and putting valuables in a deposit box at the bank.

Maslow's *third step* includes goals concerning our social involvement, especially relations with children and other family members, or with our close friends. Those third-level goals are directed at making us feel a close part of a group. We need the feeling of "belonging" or being needed.

The *fourth stage* is that level at which we should aim to feel good about ourselves. Jesus reminded us not only to "love your neighbor" but to "*love him as yourself.*" Ted Engstrom describes this as "feeling good about being you!" We cannot love somebody else as we should until we learn to love ourselves.

Finally, at Maslow's pinnacle, is what he terms "self-actualization." It is at this highest level that he sounds almost like the New Testament. Here we become so free in our goal-setting that we are no longer concerned just with ourselves. We actually give ourselves away! "Anyone who keeps his life for himself," says the Lord, "shall lose it; and anyone who loses his life for me shall find it again" (Matt. 16:25, TLB).

"This," according to Rollo May, is "a dying to part of oneself often followed by a heightened awareness of life, a heightened sense of possibility."

1. *Giving yourself away*

Each of us at some time in life has felt the thrill of being on a winning team. The bruises and scratches were forgotten in the euphoria of fighting for others and for the whole. Even self-glory was submerged—the team and its cause were everything. But higher—much higher is the triumphal submersion of self in some cause for the glory of God—the care of a refugee family by your church, the feeding of many hungry people at a rescue mission, or some other warm deed in the name of Christ.

One of the thrilling moments of my life occurred in 1965 when

I met Mother Theresa of Calcutta and observed the work of her mission. It moved me to see her take a dying woman's hand and say, "I love you, dear sister. I love you. Jesus loves you."

Called the "Saint of the Gutters," she has rescued thousands of babies from the garbage heaps, cared for hopeless lepers, and comforted the dying. She firmly believes the words of Christ, "Inasmuch as ye have done it unto one of the least of these my brethren, ye have done it unto me" (Matt. 25:40, KJV).

Born in 1910, the daughter of Albanian shopkeepers, she early heard God's call to India. Her first twenty years were spent in Calcutta where she taught wealthy girls at St. Mary's High School. But one night, while riding the night train from Darjeeling, she heard the Lord's call again—this time to assist the deprived of Calcutta. "It was," she said, "a call within a call. I was to leave St. Mary's and help the poor while living among them."

She changed her dress to a white Indian sari and, walking barefoot, made her way through Calcutta's poorest sections. There she found thousands of hungry people dwelling on the city pavements. Relying only on small cash gifts and donated foodstuffs, she fed the poor on the streets until Calcutta City gave her a run-down hotel. "I depend on God's hand," she said. Soon twelve other dedicated sisters joined her, and her work grew marvelously, enriched by her humility.

At sixty-nine, Mother Theresa was awarded the 1979 Nobel Peace Prize for her continuing dedication in loving the poor. The citation read: "This year the world has turned its attention to the plight of children and refugees . . . for whom Mother Theresa has worked for many years so selflessly."

She has given herself away for half a century—and she has found herself.

Concerning her kind of person, Meister Eckhardt wrote in 1327, "God does not give a gift so that a person may keep it and take satisfaction in it. Each gift is given so that He might give one more gift—himself. Therefore, look through every gift and every event to God and never be content with the thing itself."

2. *Setting time goals*

Anyone who is fifty or older has probably long since decided the set of his sail for life. But there are many goals within goals that need continual and timely reassessment. To do this you might periodically want to:

a. Re-evaluate your existing involvements. ("Am I achieving the things I want most to achieve in life? What should I change to reach these goals?")

b. Make a checklist of how you use your time. ("What do I do in each hourly segment of the day?")

c. Make a day-calendar of how you use each twenty-four-hour segment for a whole week. ("Am I doing enough in a week to advance my most important objectives and desires? Or am I allowing myself to be waylaid by many minor tasks?")

d. Examine your monthly calendar and make a cross-reference to see if your grand goals are being promoted consistently. ("Am I keeping score on clear advances? What specific things have I done that bring me a few steps closer to my goal?")

Pablo Picasso had many moral failings and he has been rightly criticized for them. "But," as Ellen Goodman says, "for ninety-one years he did do something remarkable. He stayed interested." His planning must have been phenomenal, and his record speaks for itself. In his lifetime he produced 14,000 canvases, 100,000 prints and engravings, and 34,000 book illustrations.

Yet through it all, Picasso was continually adjusting. He modulated his goals and objectives with numerous eras: his classical introduction, his blue period, his impressionistic interlude, his cubism and others were all pure Picasso. He was often discouraged in life, yet continually reassessing his work. He was anything but a failure with his art even in later life. Yet he plugged away as though each phase was a new experiment. Knowing his own limitations, he refused to be canonized as an artistic saint.

Every person, according to Shakespeare, has his moment on life's stage and then must step back into obscurity, old age, and death. But when such shadows threaten, we are so success-oriented in the Western world that it is hard to accept this laying aside. Picasso avoided such obscurity to the end. He arose early each morning, almost paralyzed by pessimism, but having goals clearly in mind. Even at ninety, he could still say, "Creation is the only thing that interests me."

Goodman comments on this with approval: "There is something," she says, "not sad but remarkable in his refusal to 'act his age,' or to retire gracefully. Surrounded by his own collection . . . he must have known his limits. But of compulsion or conviction, he kept working."

3. Deciding when to decide

Daniel Wheeler and Irving Janis have written helpful hints indicating ways we can get off dead-center:

a. *Accept the challenge:* "Decision-making begins when people are confronted with a challenge to their current course of action."

b. *Search for alternatves:* (1) Consider your present goals; (2) Use this information in fine-tuning or even changing some of them.

c. *Weigh the alternatives:* Seek facts and forecasts of success about each alternative.

d. *Commit yourself to a particular course of action:* Re-examine all the gathered data in planning how to put your decision into action.

e. *Once the new decision is set in motion:* Anticipate setbacks, prepare to deal with failures and continually re-plan to make the decision more concise and successful.

One of my favorite radio personalities for many years was Lowell Thomas. I recall his cheery, "Hello, everybody!" and "So long until tomorrow," from the late 1920s. He died at eighty-nine, and although grayer and slower moving, he retained the same smooth, vigorous voice. His new show was called "The Best Years" and was heard five nights a week on 250 stations. He gave brief vignettes of famous people he had known—John D. Rockefeller, Connie Mack, Henry Ford, Bob Hope, and others.

His show was the result of committing himself to a new course of action. "Here I am in my eighty-ninth year," he said, "and I'm basically starting a new career." But he based his decision to launch this show on facts and forecasts that indicated success: "The population of older people is so large, so vast," he reported, "and they're accomplishing so much, that many should listen."

His whole life had been a planned path of wise decisions. Owning stock in a number of ski resorts, he was also a large shareholder in Capital Cities Communications which operates thirteen radio and TV stations. Always interested in America's heroes, he had just published his fifty-fifth book—a biography of Jimmy Doolittle. Five more books were also in his forecast, the result of continual decision-making, even up to his death.

But with all his enlarging goals, there was a consistency to Lowell Thomas—a bright outlook on life. He always accented the positive. When asked what were *his* best years, he replies: "All my years were my best years!"

4. *Outline your day and week*

Most people do this informally, but have a normal daily and weekly routine that they follow. Indeed, some are a bit rigid:

7:00 / Calisthenics
7:15 / Get morning newspaper
7:30 / Take dog for a walk
8:00 / Breakfast with eggs over light, dry toast, black coffee
8:30 / Brisk walk to drugstore to gossip
8:40 / Ditto to hardware store for gossip
8:50 / Return to read newspaper—starting with crossword puzzle, etc., etc.

Most of us might soon go crazy following a schedule like this!

My mother-in-law, into her eighties, would say each night at exactly 10:00, "Well, I'm late to bed. Be sure to lock up."

A biographer of the great philosopher, Immanuel Kant, records this account:

"His life passed like the most regular of verbs. Rising, coffee-drinking, writing, lecturing, dining and walking," he wrote, "each had its set time. When he appeared at the door of his house and strolled toward the small avenue of linden trees, the neighbors all knew that it was exactly half-past three of the clock. So he promenaded up and down during all seasons. And when the weather was gloomy or the gray clouds threatened rain, his old servant Lampe was seen plodding anxiously after, with a large umbrella under his arm, like a symbol of Prudence."

Kant was so slight physically that he was forced to take extreme measures to schedule himself. Apparently he felt it was safer to do this without a physician—and lived to be eighty. In his seventieth year he wrote an essay entitled, "On the Power of the Mind to Master the Feeling of Illness by Force of Resolution." In it he described how it was better to breathe only through the nose—especially when one was out of doors. As a result, when he was walking in the spring, fall or winter, he allowed no one to talk to him so he would not have to answer; he felt it was better to walk silently than to have a cold.

He even had a plan to hold up his stockings each day. This he did with cloth bands that passed from the stockings through a small hole in his pockets and were tied to strings attached to little boxes.

He thought out carefully everything he did before he made a decision. Because of this he remained a bachelor all his life. At one time he thought about getting married, but he planned so long about how to ask the girl that she married someone else. On another occasion, he considered the matter again and chose another lady. But once more he spent too much time working on his proposal plan and she moved to Koenigsberg.

Despite this obvious overplanning, however, Kant produced his greatest work when he was fifty-seven. One of mankind's great masterpieces, *The Critique of Pure Reason*, both startled and upset the philosophical world. His rule for planning was simple: "I have fixed upon the line which I am resolved to follow. I will enter on this course and nothing shall prevent me from pursuing it!"

Most of us, however, fall somewhere in between the over-organization of Immanuel Kant and the under-organization of Fibber McGee's closet. Edward Dayton and Ted Engstrom suggest a system of Daily Time Inventories. These inventories break time into half-hour segments from 7:00 a.m. to 10:00 p.m.; it is suggested that one be made for each day of the week. At first, the purpose of this is not so much to determine what one *should* do as to record what one *is* doing with one's time.

For the next step, these authorities have designed a weekly calendar composed of squares on which can be written appointments for each of the seven days. This is reserved for main events only so that one can determine their suitability ahead of time. These two schedules are termed the NOW inventories.

Next, one may wish to go through to analyze and decide things that *should* be inserted in new schedules called the THEN inventories. I highly recommend a careful study of Engstrom and Dayton's book, *Strategy for Living*.

Our dear friend, "Aunt" Lillian, has squeezed an amazing degree of accomplishment into ninety years. My wife and I first met her a quarter century ago when she was chairperson of a Methodist parsonage committee. She was the first to welcome us to a church on Long Island's north shore. We had been feeling very lost and forlorn, but when she put warm arms around us, we knew that all was well. The kitchen shelves were well-stocked with food and a hot dinner awaited us on the table.

We have since tried to analyze how Lillian and her sister Sue did so many deeds of kindness in each twenty-four-hour span. They ran the church fellowship suppers, sewed exquisite doll clothing, and daily visited the sick and aged—Lillian herself was in her late sixties at the time. Her ministry to the aged usually included delicious pies, stews or soups with each visit. She is now in her nineties and the schedule that she faithfully followed for forty years has been reproduced below.

6:00 / Breakfast.
7:00 / Housecleaning.
8:00 / Start baking pies and other foods for the aged.
8:30 / Hoe garden behind house.
9:00 / Take out pies to cool.
     Prepare bread and rolls (raised during the previous night).
9:30 / Put bread into oven and commence work on saleable sewing of doll dresses and other items.
10:00 / Take out baked goods from oven.
     Continue handwork.
12:00 / Luncheon.

1:00 / Pack car and prepare for visitation to sick and aged.
1:30 / Visitation to shut-ins, often taking some for short
   rides.
3:30-5:00 / Help with farm work next door.
5:00 / Prepare dinner.
6:00 / Dinner—often with guests.
7:00-9:30 / Recreation, reading or letter writing.
      Or, often church meetings at this time.
9:30 / Evening devotions.
10:00 / Bedtime.

On her ninetieth Christmas she sent us her annual letter, filled with love and reminiscence. One can see from her letter that her gift of helps is still active.

"I remember," she wrote, "the night I stayed with the kiddies while you were out. Marj wanted us to play games with her, but I had to refuse. I saw all those clothes in your basket that needed to be ironed. I was so pleased to help you with those."

Although her legs have weakened and she and Sue are usually confined to their house, she maintains a network of interest: "We do keep busy in our house and are so happy with it. We get pleasure with our visits on the phone and the food we can send to the sick and the old folks. So we count our blessings but have a desire to do more. At our church fair, I was able to sell a granny afghan for $25 which went to the work." Past ninety now, Lillian and Sue continue to give themselves away—and find themselves.

An unknown author has penned the joys of planned time:

Take time to work—it is the price of success.
Take time to think—it is the source of power.
Take time to play—it is the secret of perpetual youth.
Take time to read—it is the fountain of wisdom.
Take time to be friendly—it is a road of happiness.
Take time to dream—it is hitching your wagon to a star.
Take time to love and be loved—it is the privilege of redeemed
   people.
Take time to look around—it is too short a day to be selfish.
Take time to laugh—it is the music of the soul.
Take time for God—He is life's only lasting investment.

J. M. Barrie once pessimistically said: "The life of every man is a diary in which he meant to write one story, and wrote another; and his humblest hour was when he compared the volume as it is with what he had vowed to make it." Nevertheless, a time of self-assessment such as this helps a person to put himself on a wiser course.

Smiley Blanton, a Christian psychiatrist, tells about a sixty-eight-year-old widower. When his wife died, he felt that life was over. But in discussing it with him, Blanton discovered the man's great love for golf. In a flash of inspiration, Blanton suggested, "Have you ever thought of establishing a golf driving range?"

The man brightened at the thought. He looked over his bank book and, with some friendly help, made plans to set up such an enterprise. At the time of the story, the man had moved to a southern town, established a golf range, and was having the time of his life. "Today," said Dr. Blanton, "instead of being a depressed and lonely old man of seventy-three, he is vigorous, cheerful and optimistic about the future—and incidentally, he plays a good game of golf." He found a rewarding schedule, made many people happy, and enjoyed the years left to him.

Thus, planning through goal-setting helps one toward a meaningful life. But planning also involves the proper use of one's material resources. In the next chapter, we shall examine some Christian principles of budgeting.

PERSONAL PLANNING NOTES

I. In planning your own daily hours, you may want to gauge your schedule against some national retirement averages:

	National Average	Your Hours
Total hours in the day	24.0	24.0
Sleep	_____	_8._
Committed time, such as:		
Mealtimes (preparing food, eating, etc.)	3.0	_4_
Housecleaning (for some)	1.6	_1.5_
Job (for some)	7.5	_____
Care for your person	1.2	_2_
Care for others	0.2	_.5_
Leisure time, such as:		
Radio and TV	2.8	_.5_
Visiting	1.6	_.5_
Taking naps	1.4	_.5_
Reading	0.7	_1._
Other discretionary time, such as:		
Working in yard or garden	0.4	_____
Handwork	0.4	_.3_
Entertaining guests	0.3	_1._
Social activities (church, etc.)	0.2	_2._
Writing letters, diaries, etc.	0.2	_.5_
Devotions, meditation	0.1	_._
Exercise: walking, jogging, swimming, etc.	0.1	_2.5_
Excursions, outings, etc.	0.1	_._
		25.8

Having added up your hours, you will be in a better position to correct your course and schedule a goal-oriented day. (Many of the averages are tentative, so that they do not arrive exactly at the 24-hour total.)

II. Next, in planning, you may also want to evaluate your past positions and the way you feel about them. This will assist you in focusing your planning on your greatest strengths. Thus: Make a list of all your past positions and give them a rating according to your emotional, intellectual, and spiritual reaction. Use E for emotional, I for intellectual and S for spiritual:

Job	Enjoyable	Moderate	Poor
_____	_____	_____	_____
_____	_____	_____	_____
_____	_____	_____	_____
_____	_____	_____	_____
_____	_____	_____	_____
_____	_____	_____	_____

III. Now you may wish to rate jobs that you have always thought you might wish to fill in your lifetime with their ratings:

Job	Strong Desire	Wish	Just a Thought
_____	_____	_____	_____
_____	_____	_____	_____
_____	_____	_____	_____
_____	_____	_____	_____
_____	_____	_____	_____
_____	_____	_____	_____
_____	_____	_____	_____
_____	_____	_____	_____

IV. Finally you may want to think about the depth and scope of your planned work during retirement, the best half of your life:

	Yes	No

1. Is this work truly planned and goal-directed? ____✓__ ___✓__

2. Does it also give me a sense of freedom and
   spiritual fulfillment? _____ ___✓__

3. Is it planned in such a way that I will receive
   some monetary return? _____ ___✓__

4. Am I satisfied that it represents God's plan
   for my life? ___✓__ ___✓__

5. Do I have a sense of daily obligation to it? ___✓__ _____

6. Is it something I have often dreamed about? ___✓__ ___✓__

7. Does it fulfill some of my basic daily
   ego-needs? ___✓__ ___✓__

8. Am I planning it in such a way that there will
   be measurable daily results? _____ ___✓__

9. Is it regarded as a valuable vocation by
   fellow Christians and by the community at
   large? _____ ___✓__

5 / Keep Budgeting

William Allen White, Pulitzer Prize-winning editor and author, once gave a fifty-acre wooded plot as a park to Emporia, Kansas. He was seventy-five years old when he also shared his philosophy on money:

"This is the last kick in a fistful of dollars. I have tried to teach people there are three kicks in every dollar: one when you make it—and how I do love to make a dollar; one when you have it—and I have the Yankee lust for saving. The third kick is when you give it away—and the biggest kick of all is the last one!"

The best book on managing your money is the Bible. The book of Proverbs, for example, is packed with advice on how to make money through diligence, honesty and prudence. The Word of God is also filled with guideposts on saving money. And most important, it is loaded with wisdom on the stewardship of sharing.

John Wesley's life illustrates unhesitating faith in God's ability and promise to supply his needs. He counseled his early followers: "Earn all you can; save all you can; and give all you can. Spend not one pound," he said, "one shilling, or one penny to gratify either the desire of the flesh, the desire of the eyes or the pride of life. Give all you can."

In addition, Wesley cautioned his disciples against taking part in any sort of enterprise where success might be gained through cheating or overcharging. "We cannot," he wrote, "consistent with brotherly love, sell our goods above fair market price; we cannot study to ruin our neighbor's trade to advance our own." To guard our stewardship of time, tithe and talent, he composed the now-famous dictum:

Do all the good you can
By all the means you can
In all the ways you can

In all the places you can
To all the people you can
As long as ever you can.

Wesley himself carried his dedication to an extreme that few others ever have or ever would. In his life he tried to exemplify what he later asked his followers to do about money. Even as a student at Oxford, he found it possible to live on twenty-eight pounds a year (perhaps $100) and save the rest to give to the poor.

As Methodism grew he was a careful steward of the church's funds. None of it ever stuck to his own hands. When a tax collector tried to assess the amount of his silver plate during the 1770s, he said to the man, "Sir, I have two silver teaspoons here in London and two at Bristol. This is all I have at present, and I shall not buy any more while so many around me want bread!"

During his life, it is estimated that Wesley gave away almost a million dollars. And when he died, it was reported that all he left were "two silver spoons and the Methodist Church."

Through it all he taught his fellow Methodists the virtues of hard work, strict honesty, thrift and social responsibility. Little wonder that Methodists were in the vanguard of the Industrial Revolution. They were part of the backbone that formed the solid middle class of the English-speaking world.

Keeping careful account books all his life, he wrote in them toward the end of his life: "For upwards of sixty-eight years, I have kept my accounts exactly—being satisfied with the spiritual conviction that I save all I can and give all I can."

1. *Earn all you can*

Donna Winn, a New York broker, suggests some sound questions on taking inventory before retirement. Her queries center primarily on emphases similar to Wesley's first two points: earning enough money and saving enough money for latter years:

   a) *Where* do you want to retire? Earning and saving ability will have an impact on your retirement location. You may find it more costly and more troublesome to stay where you are than to move.

b) *How much income will you require?* Cost of living will very likely increase rather than decrease in the days ahead.

c) *Is it possible* for you to acquire more income for your retirement days?

d) *How careful* should you be about your investments? Should you perhaps diversify your holdings or trim your life insurance?

e) *Are you planning to simplify* your lifestyle? Many people, either retired or at the point of retirement, are reassessing their earnings and finding them inadequate for today's spiraling inflation. Between being squeezed by deflated money and bored by idleness, more and more people in their fifties and sixties are opting to remain on the job or (if retired) to return to work. New state and federal laws are making it increasingly possible for men and women over sixty-five to do this. Over twenty percent in this category have elected to remain employed—and an increasing number are receiving encouragement to return to their jobs.

A study by the Bureau of Labor statistics indicates that older men and women often are more effective on the job than are their juniors. Although there are wide variances of productivity within age groups, the Bureau concluded that older employees, on the average, produce more than younger ones.

John Stevens, a youth counselor, had retired recently only to discover that his monthly income had become woefully inadequate. At sixty-eight, his social security check provided only $300 a month and his fixed pension a mere $130—yielding an annual income of $5,160. Inflation had placed him at the poverty level. Unfortunately, he had no savings. "My food costs," he says, "were horrendous. They kept going up and up—in fact, they still are."

Out of desperation as well as boredom, John returned to work as a three-hour-a-day counselor for the local "Y." The job earned him $5,000 a year plus excitement.

A study by the Heart, Blood and Lung Institute has determined that persons retiring early have a higher mortality rate than those who remain on the job, or otherwise occupied. In a survey of four thousand employees in two tire companies, the Institute found that the death rate rose sharply three to four years after retirement. This survey concluded that death was caused as much by boredom, idleness, stringent budgets and a feeling of uselessness as any other factor.

There are some companies that have wisely adjusted to retirement shock by making work more flexible for semi-retirees. Terming this system "flex-time," they allow older employees to set their own time schedules. In this way, room is made for permanent part-time workers. The work week may also be compressed so that these employees can work less than five days. Other companies allow two part-time older workers to perform the duties of one full-time younger employee. Boredom and uselessness disappear and income is appreciably increased for these golden-age people.

One older man in Arizona tried another track. He had sold his partnership in the East and retired to the Southwest with his wife. With an income of $19,000 per year he was doing well enough, yet was bored. He played golf, swam in his pool and enjoyed his two-bedroom townhouse. "But," he said, "golf began to pall on me. After all, you can play just so much golf!" Eventually he set up an employment agency for workers over fifty-five. He found this profitable, challenging and satisfying.

Mary Heather, an enterprising seventy-five-year-old woman in New England, recently bought an abandoned hydro-electric plant along one of the region's many rivers. Her neighbors at first laughed at her for purchasing what seemed a "white elephant." It had been closed down for at least thirty years and seemed worthless. In fact, the town had planned to tear it down.

But Mary and her family kept at it. Before the energy shortage hit, the plant had begun generating electricity. Its 250-watt generator produced enough power to supply 250 houses in her area. Ultimately, it should conserve the equivalent of 2,500 barrels of oil per year—equal to an estimated $50,000 in hard cash. "Just a drop in the bucket so far," she admits. "But remember how many little dams are waiting!"

The Army Corps of Engineers agrees with her, stating that there are almost six thousand such dams in this nation, sufficient to generate at least three million kilowatt hours of electricity annually—an amount equal to the output from three nuclear plants. By her creative imagination, Mary Heather has added to her own income and has stimulated the wealth of a grateful country.

2. *Save all you can for retirement*

No matter how young a person is, it is always wise to start a savings and investment plan as soon as possible. This is especially true as one realizes that the spendable part of his income probably has increased through the years. But from another viewpoint, one must remember that one has a decreasing amount of time to compensate for any investment mistakes he has made in the past.

Also, as one's age increases, he should be more and more concerned with the matter of *security*. Speculation should be decreasingly attempted—it is a young person's game. Big risks are an extravagance in which sixty- or seventy-year-olds should indulge sparingly. For example, investment counselors suggest shifting from common stock to bonds, preferred stocks, or some form of money-market funds.

Likewise, it is probably better to move away from growth stocks to securities that give one a good return—perhaps ten, eleven percent or more. Utilities, communications or electronics might be examples of such stable investments.

It is wise to recall that while small bank accounts are essential for day-to-day needs, the more one can put into other forms of equity, the better. Well-located, income-producing real estate and solid AAA bonds illustrate this type of venture.

It is also smart to remind yourself that while life insurance is good protection, it is terrible as an investment. Melvin J. Swartz in his book, *Don't Die Broke*, tells us: "The life insurance industry spends millions on advertising to promote the image that to die without life insurance ranks with kicking your mother and stepping on the flag. It does not."

It is probably far better for one to invest in entities other than life insurance when one is planning retirement. When you bought insurance years ago, it was more likely to protect your family in the event you died too young. But by retirement time you should have placed your money in other assets—real estate, stocks, bonds, cash in the bank. They have a much higher rate of return for your day-to-day living.

A year or so before retiring, it would be good for you to take an inventory of all the assets you possess:

1) Your goods should be assessed and listed at a fair and honest current market value. Your inventory might include real estate, jewelry, valuable stamps, coins, etc.

2) Realistically list each source of income you can anticipate after retirement:
   a. Bank interest and interest from other money-market equities such as C.D.'s, T-Bills, bonds, etc.
   b. Rentals from real estate you own, or royalties from writings or inventions
   c. Social Security that both you and your spouse can expect
   d. Pensions from former employers
   e. Consultant fees you might receive from your years of experience and learning
   f. Part-time employment wages, if you plan to supplement your income in this fashion
   g. KEOGH or IRA funds from self-employment pensions
   h. Other sources of income

3) Now make a realistic and detailed list of your existing costs: food, clothing, home maintenance, medical costs, transportation, entertainment, church tithing, etc.

Having created a fairly clear picture of your present status, you can better determine what changes in lifestyle might need to be made. Where can cuts or savings be implemented? Would it be wise to move to smaller, cheaper and more maintenance-free quarters?

It would also be helpful to investigate price-saving stores and other merchandisers. Transportation could be cheaper, for one thing. Some bus lines offer a fifteen percent discount for persons over sixty. Certain airlines offer Senior Season specials on winter fares.

Newspapers and magazines (*50-plus*, *Prime Time*, *Modern Maturity* and others) advertise many special prices and special events open to senior citizens. A chain of groceries in New York is leading the way among stores that give special prices to people over sixty.

The professional organization, Home Economists in Business, recently made a survey entitled, "A Penny for Your Inflation Thoughts." Readers were asked to share ideas on money-saving methods in buying and preparing food. The responses of two hundred fifty-two typical shoppers were helpful:

- Take advantage of sales.
- Cut down on convenience foods.
- Use food coupons wisely.
- Do comparison shopping.
- Make out a shopping list; don't do impulsive buying.
- Purchase large cuts of meat and wholesale chickens; do your own butchering.
- Substitute other protein sources for meat, e.g. dairy products and soy beans.
- Plan your menus to serve more than one meal.
- Serve more of the one-dish meals or casseroles.

When asked about energy-saving these same respondents had good suggestions:

- Turn off lights when not in use.
- Use a microwave oven if you have one.
- Weather-strip your windows and put a wood stove in your fireplace.
- Avoid pre-heating your oven.
- Use a car pool whenever possible.

Another source of help is found in banks. Seeing the growing market among senior people, they are often providing such things as fee-free travelers' checks, free safe deposit boxes and free notary services. Certain fine apartment houses in some cities are catering to those between sixty and eighty. They term these "fun places" for senior adults.

Also offered are club facilities to which older folk can retreat. Some restaurants are establishing senior clubs in certain parts of the nation, even offering free orange juice and coffee surrounded by a relaxed club atmosphere. These, obviously, are all money-savers and reduce the pressure on our strained nerves and pocketbooks.

3. *Give all you can*

In his essay "The Gospel of Wealth," Andrew Carnegie expounded his viewpoint that the life story of a Christian should fall into two periods: (1) That of acquiring money; and (2) that of giving it in such a way that the surplus would be utilized for the public good. And this he attempted to demonstrate in his own life. During his first sixty years he devoted himself to gaining wealth guided by the Protestant ethic of thrift, hard work, planning and foresight. His expertise in the steel industry built up almost a half billion dollars.

During the final twenty years of his life, Carnegie carefully shared this sum for the general welfare. Selling out his steel holdings to J. P. Morgan for over $400 million, he felt it his duty to give for the good of all. After his family's needs were cared for, the wealth that remained was placed in public trust. His last will read: "This is to be administered for the benefit of the whole community." In the process, he built 2,509 free libraries, founded the Carnegie Institute of Technology, gave generously to Tuskegee Institute, erected the Temple of Peace at The Hague, and the Pan American Palace in Washington. Before he died he had given away $308 million.

Clearly none of us is an Andrew Carnegie, and we lack his tremendous resources. Nevertheless, the pattern of Christian stewardship is manifest. It is well illustrated by Watts' beautiful painting in the Tate Gallery of London. The picture portrays the body of a man who has just died. Around him lie all the things he had loved throughout life—books, music, a sword, an ermine robe, a peacock feather. But at the bottom of the painting, Watts had printed the words:

"What I spent I had;
What I saved I lost;
What I gave I have."

Carnegie's pattern of giving reflected to some degree the

thoughts of Maimonedes, the Jewish scholar of the Middle Ages who provided eight steps for giving which he termed the Golden Ladder:

1. To give reluctantly, the gift of the hand, but not of the heart.
2. To give cheerfully, but not in proportion to the need.
3. To give cheerfully, and proportionately, but not until asked.
4. To give cheerfully, proportionately and unsolicited but to put the gift into the man's hand, thus causing shame.
5. To give in such a way that the distressed may know the benefactor but not be known by him.
6. To know the subjects of our bounty but remain unknown to them.
7. To give so that the benefactor may not know those whom he has relieved, and they shall not know him.
8. To prevent poverty by teaching a trade, setting a man up in business or in some other way preventing the need for charity.

One of the best bits of advice concerning our money comes to us from the Reverend Ray Ortlund:

"Most of all, transfer all ownership of it over to God. He's the wisest Financier! He can best show you how to conserve it, so that it can be the greatest blessing and return for your investment.

"God's on your side! Relax. Surrender. Lay out your books before Him."

PERSONAL FINANCIAL CHECK LISTS

I. Before moving on to chapter 6, you may want to take several simple inventories of your personal holdings and earnings as a preliminary to future budgeting:

1. Concerning your personal net worth:

Assets	At Present	My Goal at Retirement
Cash	_____	_____
Checkbook balance	_____	_____
Savings Account	_____	_____
Other _____	_____	_____

Additional Miscellaneous		
3-month, 6-month Certificates	_____	_____
Tax refunds due you	_____	_____
Returnable deposits	_____	_____
Thrift plans, Co-op funds, etc.	_____	_____
Others _____	_____	_____

Assets Readily Liquidatable		
Cash value of life insurance	_____	_____
Longer-term Certificates	_____	_____
Bonds, Stocks, Mutual Funds	_____	_____
Loans due to you	_____	_____
Other _____	_____	_____

Fixed Assets (Fair market value)		
Equity in house(s)	_____	_____
Additional real estate	_____	_____
Your share in a business	_____	_____
Auto(s), boat(s), etc.	_____	_____
Other _____	_____	_____

Smaller Fixed Assets

Jewelry, furs, etc.   _____   _____
Furniture, appliances, etc.   _____   _____
Silverware, art, etc.   _____   _____
Stamps, coins, etc.   _____   _____
Sports equipment, hobbies, etc.   _____   _____

My Total Assets   _____   _____

2. Liabilities

Short-Term Indebtedness
(i.e., due within a year)

Charge cards   _____   _____
Other credit accounts   _____   _____
Personal indebtedness
   (short-term loans)   _____   _____
Mortgage payments (monthly)   _____   _____
Other _____   _____   _____

Long-Term Indebtedness
(beyond a year)

Loans (bank and/or policy loans)   _____   _____
Auto loans (and other)   _____   _____
Mortgage balance(s)   _____   _____
Other _____   _____   _____

Total Liabilities and Indebtedness

                                           _____   _____

Balance of My Net Worth   _____   _____

(Subtract your debts and liabilities from assets to arrive at balance of net worth.)

II. It might also be helpful to you to set down your monthly cash-flow (income minus expenses) to judge where you will be financially at retirement.

1. *Income*

	Monthly Now	At Retirement
Salary or wages	_____	_____
Business earnings	_____	_____
Rents and Royalties	_____	_____
Interest from savings	_____	_____
Interest from CD's, etc.	_____	_____
Interest from Bonds	_____	_____
Dividends from Stocks	_____	_____
Retirement lump grants or funds	_____	_____
Pension	_____	_____
Income from annuity	_____	_____
IRA or KEOGH accounts	_____	_____
Social Security	_____	_____
Veteran's pension	_____	_____
Other _____	_____	_____
Total Monthly Income	_____	_____

2. *Expenses*

	Monthly Now	At Retirement
House expenses		
Rent		
Mortgage (P & I)	_____	_____
Fuel and utilities	_____	_____
Supplies and maintenance	_____	_____
Property Taxes	_____	_____
Telephone	_____	_____
Other _____	_____	_____
Clothing	_____	_____
Food—at home	_____	_____
—eating out	_____	_____
Appliances	_____	_____
Furniture and furnishings	_____	_____
Taxes (Income, etc.)	_____	_____
Car payments	_____	_____
Car expenses and maintenance	_____	_____
Church and charity	_____	_____
Insurance	_____	_____

Medical and dental	_____	_____
Miscellaneous	_____	_____
Total Monthly Expenses	$_____	$_____
Cash Flow Balance	$_____	$_____

(For cash flow balance, subtract monthly expenses from monthly income).

6 / Keep Thinking

Funk and Wagnall's Dictionary defines thinking as, "To exercise the mind actively in any way: (1) to know, feel or will; (2) in a stricter sense, to exercise the intellect; (3) in the strictest sense, to exercise the comparative and constructive faculties of the intellect."

In 1928, Ernest Dimnet wrote a book entitled *The Art of Thinking*, in which he contended, among other things, that most people indeed do *not* think very much. They are often more like robots: "Do not they consist of clothes, mannerisms, formulas (listen to what you hear at the opera or at art exhibitions)? Are not their attitudes . . . copied from models approved for standardization? Are not all their lives alike? . . . We know that nineteen people in twenty do not think, but live like automata."

In our society, children probably have the most active minds, continually asking, "What? . . . Why? . . . Where? . . . How . . .?" Their young minds are constantly remembering, comparing, probing, critiquing and judging.

Dimnet tells of a little nine-year-old girl who overheard her father and two professors discussing some trivial details about art. Suddenly she interrupted the conversation with the query, "Daddy, what is beauty? What makes it?"

On another occasion he observed a youngster of ten examining an exotic stone—perhaps wondering if it would last forever. The child asked, "What is forever?" But sadly, the time comes when such a child begins to copy Father's ways and to shrug off such questions. It is the beginning of dreariness for him. "He is growing up now," we remark.

At age eighty the philosopher Karl Jaspers was still questioning. "In my mind I am still very young," he said, "and still learning. Wisdom is never fully attainable but there are ways of getting at it. . . . You must keep regular hours, have regular sleep and proper exercise and avoid trivia."

87

Occasionally in life we return to our childlike curiosity. But as we become older, we tend increasingly to accept "pat" solutions and a crop of clichés. When we reach fifty, sixty or seventy, we may have learned to look up all the answers in the back of the book and all curiosity may have vanished. The glamour and glow of thinking and creativity may be gone . . . unless we encourage creative instincts like the sculptor Louise Nevelson. She observes her surroundings with a fresh eye.

Mrs. Nevelson has representations of her art in great museums of our nation. The Phoenix Art Museum, for example, displays many of her major art works. To celebrate her eightieth birthday, a traveling show of her work has been arranged, entitled: "Louise Nevelson—the Fourth Dimension." According to Robert Frankel, assistant director of the Phoenix Museum, she is the "greatest living American sculptor."

Her working philosophy is perhaps best summed up in her thought-provoking assertion: "One doesn't stop or start repeating oneself. People who are repeating themselves are coasting, and perhaps a little dead!" According to Ed Montini of the *Arizona Republic,* "her art is full of the fragments of peoples' lives." She is continually comparing, constructing and rearranging, often dipping into her own long experience.

Although she was virtually unknown until her forties, she doesn't worry much about recognition. "I don't depend too much on my (public) reflection," she says, "or what people say of me." She just continues to work innovatively.

A display of her newer work was shown recently at a New York exhibition. Concerning this later art she says one must "throw off one's environment and build. We have to first give ourselves."

This ability is not limited to certain people. Tests have been conducted in the San Francisco area over a thirty-eight-year period. For nearly fifty mentally-active men and women the study indicated their IQ's increased steadily with the years. Dr. Jon Kangas administered the Stanford-Binet and the Wechsler Intelligence scales at various intervals in the lives of these fifty adults. As preschoolers, they had registered an average IQ of 107. Between ages thirty and forty-four, their IQ's had risen to 130. Later tests have convinced Dr. Kangas that, in the right setting and circumstances, their IQ would continue to ascend after fifty.

A distinguished gerontologist emphasizes the same point: "The average person need not expect a 'typical' deterioration of mental functioning in later years, but rather the opposite when exercised."

Mortimer Adler in his book, *Aristotle for Everybody*, subdivides the great Greek thinker's mental process into: (1) productive thinking, (2) practical thinking, and (3) theoretical thinking. Following these ancient ideas, let us look at the mechanics of the intellect as they affect the person over fifty.

1. *Thinking to produce*

By a series of comparisons, experiments and trial-and-error methods, Thomas Edison continued to think productively and to produce valuable inventions well into his eighties. When he was seventy, one of his colleagues said of his experiments: "Edison proceeded to each new undertaking, no matter how difficult, with the expectant joy of a naive child." At sixty he began work on the storage battery, a project he would not complete for ten years. With a mystical strain in him, he wrote to a friend, "I don't think God would be so unkind as to withhold the secret of a good storage battery, if a real earnest hunt were made. I'm going to hunt!"

In his first experiments, he labored with copper oxide combined with other metals and acids. His personal search led him to test hundreds of materials, always comparing, rejecting and evaluating. "Grand chemistry," he would say, "I like it best of all the sciences." He had loved it since boyhood, and now in his sixties he began gathering personnel and equipment to conduct thousands more experiments before the battery was perfected.

He displayed amazing patience and even a rare sense of humor despite repeated disappointment. "Why, man," he said to an inquiring friend, "I've got a lot of results. I know several thousand things that won't work!"

Finally in 1903, he began to test his battery by installing it in carriages equipped with small electric motors and chain drives. He kept careful records and test sheets of each trip taken by these vehicles over the rough country roads of New Jersey. He needed to know if his batteries could stand up to rough usage.

Some of his experiments on this were amusingly unorthodox but effective. Tom Robbins, the inventor of the conveyor belt, was visiting Edison in his library in 1904 when he heard a heavy object fall outside the window. A workman appeared and said, "Second floor okay, Mr. Edison." The inventor nodded and replied, "All right, try the third floor now." Edison then explained to Robbins that he was testing the durability of his batteries by having them thrown from the upper stories of his laboratory.

When production of his early batteries began, the newspapers announced that Edison, at age sixty-four, "had revolutionized the world of power." The age of stored electricity was destined to transform land travel, sea transport, farming and (regrettably) warfare.

Then years later, Edison, along with Henry Ford, Harvey Firestone and John Burroughs (the naturalist), shared an extended camping trip. Burroughs reported that Edison "appeared in the Indian summer of his life, genial, relaxed, philosophical, going off by himself to read a book at every halt, a trenchant and original thinker."

Edison had achieved success with his early inventions such as the light bulb, the motion picture, the phonograph and scores of other beneficial projects for mankind. But his busy mind worked on into his seventies and eighties. During this latter era he developed the disk phonograph, the self-starter for cars, fluoroscopes and X-ray equipment, talking pictures, and the perfection of electric cars. He was indeed one of the mountaintop geniuses of history.

"But each of us can be a genius in his own way," one professor has put it; "everyone's mind can be stretched every day."

Mortimer Adler comments, "The human mind is the principal factor in (such) production." As mankind progressed, people learned to design plans for producing useful objects. "They became abler," says Adler, "to express their productive ideas before actually materializing them by transforming matter." Sometimes a person does this also by keeping an idea in his mind rather than writing it down. Orderly planning, pushed forward by the mind, discovers and observes God's natural laws. It keeps operating until the hands have produced the object which the thinker had in mind all along.

In ancient times, God reminded Joshua that proper thinking was the path of success: "Constantly remind the people about these laws, and you yourself must think about them every day and every night so that you will be sure to obey all of them. For only then will you succeed" (Josh. 1:8, TLB).

2. *Thinking that acts*

We turn now to goal-setting which helps one decide what he wants to do. Aristotle observed that aside from infrequent irrational behavior, most people begin activity with some purpose in mind. There is a weighing of goals, a discarding of alternatives and a planned path to achieve that one aim.

Dr. Lorena Staudt has been working as a medical missionary in India for almost sixty years. Today at ninety, she still ministers with a divine sense of purpose: "It seems to be God's will that I keep going," she says at her mission in the shadow of the Himalaya mountains. "The children in my orphanage know that I love them so!"

Dr. Staudt began, according to Jay Coleman in the *Arizona Republic*, as a young teacher in the Kentucky hills. "In 1918 when the flu broke out, I cared for sixty-five people and not one died," she says. "I learned to rub their aches and pains, and I fed them soup." She also first learned rough surgery there when a boy's arm was nearly cut off in an accident. Lorena helped the local doctor set the bone straight, stitch the wound and apply a dressing. Impressed with her skill, the physician inquired where she had learned her nursing. When she admitted this was her first such experience, he and another doctor urged her to go into medicine. She earned a Doctor of Osteopathy degree from Missouri State College and was then faced with the most important decision of her life. She was offered a practice at $800 a month in Nebraska, while simultaneously challenged by a $65-a-month mission in India. In explaining why she chose India, she says, "My mother had always read to us about missionary work when I was a girl. I guess you could say it was her fault that I wanted to be a missionary!"

After serving for six-and-a-half years in northern India, she moved to the south where she shared a salary with another worker. "If I had had a normal salary, I couldn't have learned to trust God as I did," she explains. Learning to depend solely on the Lord, she once established a mission station with a mere two dollars (15 rupees).

A touching incident in 1930 had a lasting impact on Dr. Staudt. One morning her co-workers found an abandoned newborn baby in a clump of cactus. "It took me two hours to remove the cactus stickers from her little body," she recalls. "Then I raised her as my own from the time she was six hours old. Today she is happily married to an evangelist."

In later life Dr. Staudt moved to Dehra Dun near the Himalaya Mountains. Her income now totaled $40 a month from Social Security plus $35 monthly from friends in the Assemblies of God. With this she daily fed fifteen children who were either orphans or had contracted leprosy. This work grew until she found herself caring for 180 parentless youngsters, happily living there and loving her.

At seventy-six, some doctors attempted to persuade her to give up her work. "You are too old and weak," they told her. Today, fourteen years later, she is still there laboring tirelessly. "It seems to be God's will that I keep going," she reaffirms.

Eleanor Roosevelt, at age seventy-five, explained how she kept going and thinking so effectively: "Part of it is in not getting too self-absorbed. This becomes more and more important as one gets older. Inevitably there are increasing aches and pains, and if you pay attention to them, the first thing you know, you're an invalid."

Aristotle said, regarding human thinking, that it always acts with some good purpose in mind and something that he or she wishes to get or own. "He identifies an 'end' being aimed at with a good that is desired," says Adler. This is borne out by the Apostle Paul's words: "Forgetting what lies behind me and straining to what lies before me, press on to the goal for the prize of God's high call" (Phil. 3:13, 14, Moffatt).

3. *Thinking for its own sake*

Elizabeth Cless is the administrator for a UCLA branch of the Plato Society. This national federation of seminars is designed primarily for older professionals, ministering to the mental needs of those who feel intellectually cut off. She says, "Their children are likely to be grown and off somewhere, moved away to follow careers of their own . . . their friends retiring, or dying. They have been in the same social circle for years and know what Charlie is going to say before he says it." It is for folks like these that a program has been established in different parts of the country.

The curriculum, found in various universities, concentrates on inner-directed studies: Members of the program, reports Ursula Vils in the *Los Angeles Times*, can choose from a variety of subjects such as:

1) Aging: developmental aspects of adulthood in its various phases.
2) Implications of multi-media and their effect on the American public.
3) A study of Andean and Mayan cultures of the fourth to the tenth centuries as compared with the Mediterranean world of the same periods.
4) Alternative energy: with a study of solar, geothermal, nuclear and other sources of energy generation.

The group invites resource people—mainly professors—to come and lecture in forty-five-minute periods on topics that interest and excite them. Among those retired people who study at the Plato Society are medical doctors, former professors, college presidents, retired judges, photographers, teachers, social workers and anyone else challenged by topics of this sort.

In time, these people themselves are used as lecturers to be exchanged with groups around the nation. Harvard and U.C. Berkeley, among other schools, share programs of this sort and are regularly participating in exchanges.

One man, a retired druggist, testifies to the helpfulness of the program: "As a professional student, I took a technical course in pharmacy. In those days there were no pre-pharmacy courses, so I missed out on all the academic subjects. I want to get these for myself now, and also so that I can talk intelligently at my son's and daughter's homes when they are entertaining."

Dr. Belle Beard, writing in the *Journal of Gerontology*, found that people such as these who read and study regularly actually improve with age. Those who do not exercise their minds go downhill. The continuous use of our minds and bodies is the most important factor in aging successfully. Thus, the more we use our minds the brighter and happier we will be.

Aristotle says, "Thinking begins with the formation of ideas on the basis of information received by our senses . . . [but] thinking goes further. It relates the ideas it produces. It joins them together, separates them, and sets one idea against another." Thinking can be exhilarating! Like a highly sensitive computer the mind stores, classifies, distinguishes, collates and concludes. Its conclusions are retained in categories and subcategories for future use. Its memory bank is enormous and far more sophisticated than the finest data processing equipment.

The mind can also absorb information from sense experience (seeing, touching, etc.) and apply it in special sciences. "By the further activities of thinking," says Adler, "the mind produces knowledge of objects that do not fall within our sense experience. Arithmetic, algebra and geometry are good examples of such knowledge."

One of the finest instances of the maturing mind was that of Benjamin Franklin who at age sixty-nine created a mountain of intellectual achievements:

1) Writing the Plan of Union (for the birthing of the United States).
2) Laying the groundwork for the Articles of Confederation.
3) Helping the new country to begin printing paper money.
4) Aiding in the establishment of the Continental Army.
5) Organizing our earliest postal system.
6) Co-drafting the Declaration of Independence.

Then, at age seventy, Franklin was sent to Paris as our first ambassador to France. With tact, patience, courtesy, and, above all, intellectual brilliance, at age seventy-two he completed a treaty of alliance with France that assured eventual victory for the American Revolution. When he was seventy-seven, he helped to draft the Treaty of Paris that gave the former colonies everything they could hope for.

Returning to Philadelphia at seventy-nine, he became President of Pennsylvania, an office now termed "governor." Manasseh Cutler, a scientist from Massachusetts, gives us a glimpse of the aged but alert Franklin at the age of eighty-one:

"I met a short, fat, truncheoned old man in a plain Quaker suit with a bald pate and short white locks sitting hatless under a mulberry tree in his Philadelphia garden.

"He arose from his chair, took me by the hand, expressed his joy at seeing me and begged me to seat myself close beside him. His voice was low, but his countenance open, frank and pleasing."

After dark, Franklin took Cutler to his study, "A very large chamber and high-studded. The walls were covered with bookshelves filled with books; beside these are five large alcoves filled in the same manner." Cutler described Franklin's well-used book supply as "the largest and by far the best private library in America."

The great philosopher also showed Cutler some of his many inventions (some devised in his old age): "a glass machine for exhibiting the circulation of blood in the arteries and veins of the human body; the rolling press which Franklin had invented for copying letters; his long artificial arm and hand for taking down and putting up books on high shelves; his great armchair with rockers (the rocking chair was also a Franklin invention); and a large fan placed over the chair with which he fans himself and keeps off the flies while he is reading; and many other inventions, all his own."

Cutler concluded the report on his visit: "I was highly delighted with the extensive knowledge he appeared to have on every subject, the brightness of his memory, and the clearness and vivacity of his mental faculties, notwithstanding his age."

Ernest Dimnet summarizes several vital lessons in thinking, lessons that he sees in the example set by such men as Franklin:

1) To review one's knowledge regularly.
2) To reflect on one's knowledge.
3) To write down one's thoughts as he progresses.

4) To preserve one's best thoughts in books and documents.
5) To read the best books.
6) To compare one's best thoughts with other men's discoveries.

Marcus Aurelius, the great Roman emperor and thinker, said: "A man's life is what his thoughts have made him." And an American sage seconded the idea with the words: "A man is what he thinks about all day long."

An unknown poet has described the power of the mental process in a poem:

"I hold it true that thoughts are things
Endowed with body, breath and wings,
And that we send them forth to fill
The world with good results or ill.

"That what we call our secret thought
Flies to the earth's remotest spot,
Leaving its blessings or its woes
Like tracks behind it as it goes."

But since medicine, psychology and the Bible remind us that we must maintain a "sound mind in a sound body," let us next examine ways for maintenance of a healthy physical constitution.

As a summary to this chapter, you may wish to review your thinking and learning processes; inventorying methods for keeping your mind active before and after retirement. Work sheets follow for this purpose.

A. *Reading* (state the number of
books in each category listed
below)

	Monthly Now	Monthly at Retirement
1. *Recreational Books*		
Fiction	_____	_____
Sports	_____	_____
Travel	_____	_____
Games	_____	_____
Other _____	_____	_____
2. *Method Books* ("How to Books")		
Prayer and spiritual life	_____	_____
Family books	_____	_____
Financial help	_____	_____
Emotional well-being	_____	_____
Health	_____	_____
Diet	_____	_____
Other _____	_____	_____
3. *Magazines/Periodicals*		
Current events	_____	_____
Housekeeping	_____	_____
Fiction	_____	_____
Financial	_____	_____
Informational	_____	_____
Intellectual	_____	_____
Entertainment	_____	_____
Spiritual	_____	_____
Other _____	_____	_____
4. *Thought-Stimulating Books*		
Bible Studies	_____	_____
Theological	_____	_____
Philosophical/Logical	_____	_____
Historical	_____	_____
Scientific	_____	_____
Other _____	_____	_____
Total books read or planned:	_____	_____

(score for reading: 0- 3 = needs improvement
                      4-12 = good
               13-20 = superior)

B. *Study Plans* (list number of school courses, informational projects, adult education, etc.)

	Every Six Months Now	Every Six Months at Retirement
Adult Education Courses	_____	_____
Personal Study Projects	_____	_____
School/College or Bible Courses	_____	_____
Travel Seminars	_____	_____
Pursuit of College Degree or other Diploma	_____	_____
Bible Study Groups	_____	_____
Language Study	_____	_____
Other _____	_____	_____

C. *Mental Problem-Solving* (Answer Yes or No)

	Now	At Retirement
Have you a daily/weekly think-time established?	_____	_____
Have you a personally effective think-method?	_____	_____
Do you use short-range planning in it?	_____	_____
Long-range planning?	_____	_____
Other _____	_____	_____

D. *Improvement of Methods in Your Own Thought-Analysis*

	O.K. As Is	Needs Working On
1. Your method of gathering data/information	_____	_____
2. Dividing or dissecting your thoughts	_____	_____
3. Classifying thoughts into subheadings	_____	_____
4. Assigning priorities to various steps in thinking process	_____	_____
5 Reaching solutions	_____	_____

6. Diagnosing complexities   _____   _____
7. Putting your ideas into a
   system   _____   _____
8. Perceiving similarities/
   differences   _____   _____
9. Filtering/screening ideas   _____   _____
10. Reviewing/recapping
    thoughts   _____   _____
11. Other _____   _____   _____

E. *Providing a Personal Think-Tank*

1. Setting goals for a specific thought-subject:
   Goal 1 _____
   Goal 2 _____
   Goal 3 _____

2. Providing sources and resource-persons for thought solu-
   tion:
   Source 1 _____
   Source 2 _____

3. Steps needed for thought-solution:
   Step 1 _____
   Step 2 _____

4. Deadlines for solutions of each step:

	Deadline	Finished
Solution for Step 1	_____	_____
Solution for Step 2	_____	_____

5. *Starting Some Final Thought-Solutions*
   Solution 1_____
   Solution 2_____
   Solution 3_____

7 / Keep Healthy

Claude Pepper, eighty-year-old congressman from Florida, is now chairman of the U.S. House Committee on Aging. He says, "You have reached old age when you need your glasses to find your glasses, or when people say you're looking good, but not that you're good-looking, or when you think today's policemen look like kids."

As the years pass, a person's interests change and sometimes lag, especially if they are failing physically. But psychological studies indicate that those very ailing bodies may actually be the *result* of ailing attitudes. Investigations demonstrate that our lagging interests may indeed be the cause of many bodily disfunctions. When we allow dullness and humdrum to take over our lives, our bodies respond with listless eyes, poor appetites and careless physical habits.

Dr. Arnold Hutchnecker asks, "How many musical instruments, how many collections and handcraft tools, how many skis, skates and balls, books, records and albums are gathering dust in your attic? How many arts and skills are withering inside of you, not from aging but from neglect?"

Many of us surrender not only the brashness of the young, but its enthusiasm as well. We often lay aside the adventures of youth, and that is the time when our muscles can start to grow fatty tissue.

One seventy-seven-year-old lady is an example of vivacity for all of us. She keeps healthy with positive attitudes and habits. "I take care of myself," she says, "I eat right, my blood pressure isn't too high, and I don't get sick an awful lot. I don't take medicine and I rarely get a headache."

When her husband died after fifty-two years of marriage, she joined a health club. She exercises, walks and runs regularly. "I put on my leotards," she laughs, "and I don't look half bad for an old lady!" She attributes her health partially to sensible eating and partially to the exercise at her health club. She bicycles, jogs, stretches, twists and lifts weights.

Her doctor agrees with her. "Whatever you're doing," he says, "keep doing it. You have so much energy, you could be a football player!"

After exercising for an hour and a half three times a week, she does interesting things. She crochets, sews and does her own yard work. Then she shops, sits with sick friends and assumes an important role in the American Businesswomen's Association. She is currently helping to plan for their national convention.

Undoubtedly, this lady's beautiful golden years are due to her Christian outlook on life. "I'm a contented person," she smiles, "with a lot of marvelous friends. With my faith I also have the Lord's basic philosophy, 'Do unto others as you would have them do unto you.' " She also says she doesn't require more insurance. When a salesman calls, she tells him, "I don't need more insurance because when I die, I'm going to die running!"

1. *Keep exercising*

When we stop exercising, our bodies speed their aging. Physicians tell us that there is *no* age at which we should become physically idle. "We keep our bodies young," says Dr. Hutschnecker, "not by putting intermittent violent strain on them, but by using them habitually in enjoyable physical activity." Dr. Harry Benjamin in *American Medicine* magazine affirms this: "The problem," he advises, "is not to add years to your life, but to add life to your years."

Walking and swimming are among the healthiest and least strenuous of all exercises. One needs to find his own optimum. If a person has had little exercise most of his life, he should take it easy when he begins exercising. The lungs, muscles and heart need a chance to build up endurance. If someone has a physical handicap or ailment, he should consult his doctor as to the best and most appropriate exercise. But remember that it is never too late to start.

Routine walks to market, chores at home or office can be occasions for flexing the arms, legs, fingers and feet. Walking on tiptoe through a simple chore can exercise long-unused muscles. Dr. Rufino Macagba used to tell our World Vision training programs, "Remember, your legs are your second heart! So keep them pumping and you will improve your circulation and your health." My wife and I walk at least a mile a day and swim ten to fifteen laps in our community pool. When we neglect this daily exercise our bodies miss it and we feel the difference in lessened vitality.

Dr. Ralph Paffenberger of Stanford University School of Medicine conducted a study showing that as physical exercise increased in an experimental group, the number of heart attacks decreased dramatically. His findings also revealed that those who used up less than 2,000 calories per week were sixty-four percent more likely to have coronary attacks than those who used up over 2,000.

In order to consume 2,000 calories weekly, for instance, a person could walk briskly about forty-five minutes a day. Or if swimming is preferred, one should use the crawl or breast stroke at least one-half hour a day. Moderate tennis will expend the same 2,000 calories at the rate of 35 minutes a day. Jogging at five and a half miles per hour requires 40 minutes daily to consume the necessary calories.

Whatever exercise you use will increase the heartbeat and cause you to breathe more deeply. Even leading an imaginary orchestra will lengthen your life if you do it regularly. Pablo Casals was directing at age ninety-four, Leopold Stokowski at eighty-three, and Arthur Fiedler at eighty-five. Using a pencil as a baton, one can turn on the phonograph with favorite music and enjoy a half hour's exercise in conducting. It's fun, will raise your spirits and use up your calories.

But don't expect exercise alone to achieve good health. One needs a balance of exercise, good food, and Christian faith. "Strive," says Dr. Harry Johnson, "for a sense of well-being with or without flawless health." Exercise retards the development of arteriosclerosis and guards against heart disease. It promotes proper nourishment of the body tissues and ensures better oxygen supply to all the organs. This results in more youthful vitality. The key word, say the doctors on exercise, is "moderation."

Such exertion also improves one's spirits. One institute of gerontology, has conducted a study on some people with an average age of sixty-six. All those involved had been suffering from mental depression. The inquiry found that their anxiety was vastly diminished after a program of swimming, running or brisk walking. Each testified to being more relaxed, more self-confident and more optimistic after regular exercise for several months. They all had regained a "taste for life."

The *New York Times* reported on a recent study on walking at the University of Tel Aviv. "Walking is best suited," they said, "for people who are out of shape, are not athletic, or who have long been sedentary." It also helps to improve physique and keep one fit even among those who *are* in top condition. Researchers at the University commented on the various advantages of walking:

1. *Walking is easy.* Except for a few basic suggestions, it requires no particular preparation or capacity.
2. *Walking is convenient.* No season of the year inhibits walking. One can walk almost anywhere. And it is the best exercise to fit into your daily schedule.
3. *Walking is economical.* All you need is your regular clothing and a pair of comfortable shoes. No other equipment is required.
4. *Walking is available to just about everybody.* This is true even of those in advanced years. People with medical difficulties like arthritis, heart trouble or emphysema can also walk to improve their health.

Dr. Lenmore Zohman of Montefiore Medical Center says, "Walking is terrific exercise. It's rehabilitative, it's preventive and it's simple. But it's under-used." According to a book written by her and Drs. Kaddus and Softness: "Walking can help you lose weight. A three-mile walk in an hour's time by a 160-pound person uses up about 285 calories."

According to a study at the Pennsylvania College of Podiatric Medicine, the average American will walk about 115,000 miles during his lifetime based on the average longevity of 73.3 years and the average daily walk of 4.3 miles a day (including all activities in office, home and elsewhere). This means that figures have increased from 70,000 miles per person in a lifetime derived from previous studies.

Dr. Fred A. Stutman, in his volume *The Doctor's Walking*

Book, urges us to walk for an hour at least four days a week. He suggests spreading out our walking over each day: "You don't have to spend your hour all at once. Think of it as a dollar bill. For example: Fifteen minutes morning and evening, to and from work, and a half hour at lunch time add up to the same results as one full hour at a time."

Even Ralph Waldo Emerson had a good word for walking: "Endurance, plain clothes, old shoes, an eye for nature, good humor, vast curiosity, good speech, good silence, and nothing too much." Emerson lived into his eightieth year.

Dr. Herbert DeVries, an exercise physiologist, reports that walking slows down the damaging effects of aging such as bone deterioration and substitution of fat for muscle tissue. It assists you in reducing hypertension and can even alleviate your headaches. It is a medicine for your mind as much as for your body. It relieves depression or anger and allows you to daydream or solve problems.

Some people are more ambitious, hankering for strenuous walking. One man, an *Arizona Republic* reporter in his sixties, recently decided to hike into the Grand Canyon. First, however, he got himself in shape by weeks of bicycling and walking. Ready to go, he donned his backpack and headed into the canyon. On the trek he met a vivacious band of oldsters:

"A happy, talkative group of seventeen senior citizens was hard to ignore. The oldest was seventy-three; the youngest was sixty-seven—on her day-pack was a beautiful flower that her grandchildren gave her for the hike. That night she wore it to dinner at the ranch in the canyon."

It was tougher for those who were unprepared or inexperienced hikers. In the early morning the writer heard amidst groans, "Somebody switched my legs on me during the night. I can't move!"

A humorous lesson for us all. Prepare yourself with slowly increasing degrees of intensity. Practice regularly and do things in moderation. You will be the better for it.

2. *Observe suitable habits*

The American Medical Association advertises good health by

a display with this heading: "Seven Good Habits Your Doctor Wishes You Had."

1. Three meals a day
2. Moderate exercise
3. Adequate sleep
4. No smoking
5. Immunization
6. Moderate weight
7. Alcohol in moderation (if indeed, at all)

Dr. Lester Breslow, dean of UCLA.'s Public Health Department, recently conducted studies on the success of these medical rules. One of his concluding comments was: "A man at age fifty-five who follows all seven good habits has the same physical health as a person twenty-five to thirty years younger who follows less than two of the health practices. Following these seven rules will add at least eleven years to a man's life."

It is in Transcaucasia that we find such rules for living best demonstrated. Here in a 750-mile strip of mountains overlooking the Caspian Sea, mankind has achieved his greatest longevity. The dwellers, called Abkhazians, live in a rugged but healthy high country which they call "God's Afterthought."

Their daily schedule is as regular as clockwork and their diet is simple and nourishing. As a result, many Abkhazians live into their nineties and a surprising number survive to ages well over one hundred.

One of these centenarians greeted a stranger with the words, "May you live as long as Moses!" The speaker himself proved to be nearly one hundred twenty. These rugged people pursue activities without worry or inner stress; they live vigorous lives. They possess a lifelong sense of usefulness and persist in daily chores to the end of their days.

"Every day is a gift," one centenarian observed, "when you are over one hundred." Another man, about one hundred and ten, credited his longevity to bathing daily in the brisk mountain streams. These hardy folk rise and retire with the sun, and observe extremely regular habits. Their food, free of fatty substances and salt, is simple and nutritious. Surprisingly, they survive exceedingly well on a mere 1700 to 1900 calories daily.

In the high country of Ecuador another group of long-lived people, called *longevos*, exhibit similar habits and diets. A medical team from the United States found men of ninety ploughing alongside others half their age. Many women of one hundred or over were weaving cloth or working in the bakeries. Men of ninety-five were busily treading clay to make adobe. Yet the physicians discovered no evidence of heart trouble or other serious diseases. Steady physical work habits seemed to be a vital element in their long lives. Instinctively they seemed to observe AMA's seven good health rules.

The medical teams confirmed that their frugal diets, good climate and quiet lives were basic factors among the *longevos*. While they maintained active lives, they gave up worries, breathed deeply of the fresh mountain air and drank much of the clear brook water. A journalist from *El Telegrafo* of Lima cites low stress as the reason for their long lives: "No trouble, no strain. That's their secret."

Writing to the Thessalonian Christians, the Apostle Paul told the same secret: "This should be your ambition: to live a quiet life, minding your own business and doing your own work" (1 Thess. 4:11, TLB).

3. *Keep eating properly*

The American Association of Retired People suggests three simple meals a day (with perhaps two very simple snacks). Such a menu for one day might be:

For breakfast:
one egg (three times a week)
or
nourishing wheat cereal or oatmeal
two slices of whole wheat toast
a glass of low-fat milk, mild coffee (1 cup)
or mild tea (1 cup)

For midmorning snack:
orange juice or
a half grapefruit

For lunch:
tuna fish or fruit salad
raw vegetables
a glass of low-fat milk

For midafternoon snack:
a cup of cold vegetable soup or consommé
whole wheat crackers
a cup of mild tea

For dinner:
stewed chicken or another lean meat
green vegetables
lettuce salad

"Our diet," says Dr. Marc Weksler of the Cornell Medical Center's Geriatric Center, "obviously has a tremendous impact on the way we age." Weksler has found through extensive experimentation that low-calorie diets greatly extend youth. As indicated in the previous section, the *longevos* and Abkhazians did well on 1700 to 1900 calories daily, many living into their eighties, nineties, or even into their hundreds.

The Food and Nutrition Board of the National Academy of Sciences recommends a daily 2400-calorie diet for a 154-pound (5-foot 7-inch) man and a 1700 calorie diet for a 128-pound 5-foot 2-inch) woman.

The Council divides the diet into four basic groups, all of which should be balanced in a daily schedule:

1. *The meat group*: Two servings daily of lean meat, poultry or fish (an egg may be substituted for a meat serving three times a week)
2. *The vegetable group*: Four servings of green vegetables daily
3. *The milk group*: Two servings of low-fat milk, low-fat cheese or yogurt (ice cream can be served occasionally)
4. *The bread-cereal group*: Four servings daily of a whole wheat or whole grain preparation such as whole wheat cereals, crackers, or bread, oatmeal or natural rice

The *longevos* of Villacamba eat a 1900-calorie diet of grain, soup, corn, yucca root, beans or potatoes. They also consume generous amounts of fruits such as oranges and bananas. Meat is scarce for them; they average only an ounce of it per week. Herb tea is their major beverage.

The Abkhazians of Transcaucasia eat large quantities of fruit and green vegetables with some chicken and goat meat. They also enjoy much yogurt and buttermilk. Eighty percent of their calories, however, are derived from the vegetable group, and the fat content of their meats and cheeses is reported to be very low.

One is reminded of the test suggested to Nebuchadnezzar's diet superintendent by Daniel and his friends: "Daniel made up his mind not to eat the food and wine given to them by the king." The dietitian was alarmed by Daniel's idea: "I'm afraid," he said, "you will become pale and thin." To allay his fears, Daniel suggested a ten-day diet of only vegetables and water. By the end of that period, the food supervisor could see how they looked. The result was a clincher: "At the end of the ten days, Daniel and his three friends looked healthier and better nourished" than the others who had eaten the king's rich foods and wine (Dan. 2:8, 10, 15, TLB).

God has given us sensible dietary needs and those who are wise will follow them.

4. *Keep unnecessary stress low*

Dr. Hans Selye of the University of Montreal says, "Stress is the spice of life that puts us to work and makes us productive." It is clear that living involves some stress, that stress is an essential dimension of living. In fact, Selye even dedicated one of his books: "To those who are not afraid to enjoy the stress of a full life, nor too naive to think that they can do so without intellectual efforts."

Another psychologist has said, "Even getting up in the morning is a great cause of stress and yet we don't remain in bed."

The key words to remember, however, are *"unnecessary* stress." Such excessive mental pressure could be defined as "allowing stress to persist indefinitely or repeatedly without pursuing measures to relieve it." When we allow our minds to live in stress, we weaken our body's ability to resist. As we unnecessarily battle the same stress over and over in our fantasy, the pressure moves into the realm of *anxiety*. We thus develop a free-floating fear of *unknown disasters* that can wear down our body's glandular machinery. To fight the battle in reality is one thing, but to fight it repeatedly in our dream world takes an unnecessary toll.

"So," our Lord tells us, "don't be anxious about tomorrow. God will take care of your tomorrow too. Live one day at a time" (Matt. 6:34, TLB).

A study of almost two hundred graduates of Harvard's class of '43 followed their trials and ups and downs for thirty-seven years. At the beginning of this longitudinal study they were all rated as physically and mentally healthy. They submitted periodic reports to the study committee regarding their successes and failures and also shared records of biennial physical examinations. The records on each man listed his psychiatric problems, his use of tranquilizers, his marriage history, the pluses and minuses of his career, his recreational victories and a history of his sicknesses. By the age of fifty-three, twenty percent had died or were chronically ill. Almost all of these had scored "lowest" on attitudinal ratings eight years earlier when they were forty-five. The diagnoses or causes of death had been cancer, heart disease, hypertension, diabetes, emphysema or suicide. Only four of the men had been rated as "best" in their personal adjustments.

On the other hand, one-third of the original group (who were all listed as "best" in personal adjustment) were also rated in excellent physical shape at age fifty-three. Contrarily, among those who were considered "worst" in personality profile, it was found that their health deteriorated two-and-a-half times faster than the well-adjusted group. The decline in health was related more directly to poor emotional adjustment than any other factor. Successful or unsuccessful responses to stress seemed to be primary factors in each man's record.

All persons on earth are exposed to similar stresses, according to Dr. Hutschnecker: "A conflict with a business partner or a marriage partner, sexual dissatisfaction, illness and injury to somebody close to us, the threat of unemployment or the reality of it, death in the family, a disaster that threatens or befalls a child, all these and many more produce stress."

Dr. Thomas Holmes, professor of psychiatry at the University of Washington, has designed a scale that ranks stresses which people can undergo in a lifetime. According to his scoring method, anyone who experiences a total score of 300 or more within a year has reached a stress "danger point." A partial listing of his scale is as follows:

Stressful Situation	Score
Death of a husband or wife	100
Divorce	73
Separation in a marriage	65
Death of a near family member	63
Serious injury or illness to oneself	63
Loss of job	47
Retirement	45
Sickness of a family member	45
Difficulties with sex adjustment	44
Financial changes	39
Death of a close friend	36
Change in personal habits	24

These are just some of Dr. Holmes' stresspoints, but there are others he does not include. For example, "becoming a grandfather for the first time" would be at least 35 on my personal scale. Entering the "empty nest" rates a 40 from my wife.

But meeting and conquering these stresses is another matter. Dr. Donald Sapp, pastor of the Paradise Valley United Methodist Church, faced with the death of his first wife and the care of three teenagers, suffered severe stress problems. Sustaining him, he relates, was a fivefold recovery plan:

1. *Saturate yourself with the Bible.* He found great comfort, he reports, from the Psalms, Isaiah and the gospels. Reading the Scriptures regularly, memorizing helpful passages and meditating on them at needed times were vital to his recovery.

2. *Pray regularly.* Don states that during this time he used

God's telephone number constantly: "JER-33-3—'Call me, and I will answer you; I will tell you wonderful and marvelous things!' " (Author's paraphrase.)

3. *Share your stresses and anxieties with a group of other troubled people.* The patriarch Job was a manager of grief. He was able to *talk out* his numbness and initial shock at the loss of his children and goods. Then he *expressed his bottled-up anger.* Next he *reminisced* over the good times he recalled. Eventually, *true healing took place* when he fully met with God.

Dr. Art Ulene of NBC suggests stress groups where people under special pressure can open up and share their grief, resentment and good memories within a warm accepting social climate. Keep your family close around you in these times and don't withdraw. They understand and love you better than anyone.

4. *Keep involved in activities of real interest to you.* When the Lord was about to leave His grieving disciples, He told them through a parable, "Keep busy till I return." In the drama, *I Remember Mama*, the mother always resorted to her brush and pail when she was under stress, and scrubbed the kitchen floor. A friend who had just lost her husband in death spent a year decorating her house and keeping her garden trim and beautiful. Healing takes places as we work meaningfully.

A pastor friend who lost a daughter in an auto accident spent the next three or four months writing a beautiful book about her. Into it he poured all his love, grief, anger, prayer and poetry. In the process God healed his soul.

Albert Schweitzer, medical missionary to Africa, lived a life remarkably free of unnecessary stress. During an average day at his Lambarene hospital, even after age ninety, he attended his duties at the clinic and made his medical rounds, did strenuous carpentry, moved crates of medicine and played the organ regularly. His busy hands kept him on a life-affirming journey for ninety-five years. "I have no intention of dying," he cheerfully told his co-workers, "so long as I can do things for God. And if I keep doing things there is no need to die. So I will live a long, long time!"

5. *Be thankful.* In moments of stress this can be very difficult, but it is the key to Christian joy. How often the Apostle Paul concluded his urgings with the words, "and be thankful."

An extremely anxious man once visited Dr. Norman Vincent Peale and catalogued all of his troubles. After listening patiently for a while, Dr. Peale handed his watch to the troubled man. "Take this," he urged, "and go into the next room. Kneel by a chair, place the watch before you and for five solid minutes try to tell God everything for which you are thankful to Him. When you have finished, come back here and we will go over your troubles again." The man did as he was asked. In five minutes the door opened and out came the man with a beaming face. "Now about your troubles . . ." began Dr. Peale. But the man shook his head: "They seem to have faded," he interrupted with a happy, surprised expression.

A missionary in China related the same phenomenon many years ago. She was filled with fear and anxiety as the enemies of the Gospel encroached on her mission work. One morning her heart was so heavy that she went to the chapel to pray alone. As she looked at the sanctuary wall, she saw a motto she had read superficially many times: "Why not try thanksgiving?" Her next hour overflowed with remembrances of blessing after blessing God had poured into her life through her years of overseas service. During that hour her anxieties dissipated.

"*With thanksgiving* let your requests be made known unto God," says the epistle to the Philippians, "and the peace of God which passeth all understanding, shall keep your hearts and minds through Christ Jesus" (Phil. 4:6, 7, KJV).

After reading this chapter, you may want to assess your own health in terms of several sets of national standards. See charts on pages that follow.

I. The medical profession has devised an RQ (risk-quotient of premature death). Circle the appropriate numbers and add together for your RQ total:

1. Age	1 10-19	2 20-29	3 30-39	4 40-49	6 50-59	8 60 & over _____
2. Heredity	1 No family heart disease	2 1 relative with heart disease	3 2 relatives with heart disease	4 1 relative with heart disease under 60	6 2 relatives with heart disease under 60	_____
3. Weight (see weight chart following RQ scoring)	0 Over 5 lbs. below weight	1 −5-+ 5 of weight chart	2 6-9 lbs. over chart	3 20-34 lbs. over chart	5 35-59 lbs. over chart	7 60 or more lbs. over chart _____
4. Tobacco	0 don't use	1 cigar or pipe	2 10 cigarettes daily or less	4 20 cigarettes daily	6 30 cigarettes daily	10 40 or more _____
5. Exercise*	1 strong exercise at work/play	2 medium exercise at work/play	3 sedentary job and much exercise	4 sedentary work and light exercise	6 light and very intermittent exercise	8 total absence of all exercise _____
6. Fat in Your Diet	1 below 180 mg cholesterol diet has no animal or solid fats	2 between 181-210 mg diet has 10% fats	3 211-239 mg diet has 20% fats	4 230-254 mg diet has 30% fats	5 255-279 mg diet has 40% fats	7 281+ mg diet has 50%+ fats
			(To be determined by regular physical examinations by your physician)			_____
7. Blood Pressure (systolic)	1 100 or under	2 100-120	3 120-140	4 140-160	6 160-180	8 180-200+ _____
8. Your Age and Sex	1 Under 40 female	2 40-50 female	3 50+ female	5 Male	6 Male stocky build	7 Male stocky and bald _____

---

*The University of California at Davis' Human Fitness Laboratory has devised the following formula for gauging your ideal exercise pulse (training rate):

220 minus your age multiplied by .75 = training rate.

For a person age 65, this would mean an exercising pulse rate of 116.

One should exercise for at least one-half hour daily, three or four times a week. (Obviously one should check with his/her physician before commencing on any rigorous exercise program.)

In scoring your RQ (Risk Quotient), add up the digits in the right-hand column and rate yourself on survivability as follows:

If your total is:
  6 to 11, your risk is *much* below average
12 to 17, your risk is still below average
18 to 24, your risk is generally around average
25 to 31, your risk can be considered moderate
32 to 40, your risk is very high
41 to 62, your risk is at a dangerous level—consult your doctor!

II. *Desirable weights* for women, age 25 and older:

Height Feet/Inches	Small frame	Medium frame	Large frame
4' 8"	92- 98	96-107	104-119
4' 9"	94-101	98-101	106-122
4' 10"	96-104	101-113	109-125
4' 11"	99-107	104-116	112-128
5' 0"	102-110	107-119	115-131
5' 1"	105-113	110-122	118-134
5' 2"	108-116	113-126	121-138
5' 3"	111-119	116-130	125-142
5' 4"	114-123	120-135	129-146
5' 5"	118-127	124-139	133-150
5' 6"	122-131	128-143	137-154
5' 7"	126-135	132-147	141-158
5' 8"	130-140	136-151	145-163
5' 9"	134-144	140-155	149-168
5' 10"	138-148	144-159	153-173

For women between 18 and 25 years old, subtract one pound for each year under 25.

For men, age 25 and older:

Height Feet/Inches	Small frame	Medium frame	Large frame
5′ 1″	112-120	118-129	126-141
5′ 2″	115-123	121-133	129-144
5′ 3″	118-126	124-136	132-148
5′ 4″	121-129	127-139	135-152
5′ 5″	124-133	130-143	138-156
5′ 6″	128-137	134-147	142-161
5′ 7″	132-141	138-152	147-166
5′ 8″	136-145	142-156	151-170
5′ 9″	140-150	146-160	155-174
5′ 10″	144-154	150-165	159-179
5′ 11″	148-158	154-170	164-184
6′ 0″	152-162	158-175	168-189
6′ 1″	156-167	162-180	173-194
6′ 2″	160-171	167-185	178-199
6′ 3″	164-175	172-190	182-204

III. The following exercise chart measures the effectiveness of 10 popular sports used at least one-half hour daily or three hours per week. (Multiply the number of ½-hour days times the fitness factor.)

Sport	No. of ½-hour days per week	Fitness Factor	Your Score
Jogging	_____	× 15	_____
Bicycling	_____	× 14	_____
Swimming	_____	× 14	_____
Skating (roller or ice)	_____	× 14	_____
Skiing (cross-country)	_____	× 14	_____
Basketball	_____	× 13	_____
Tennis	_____	× 13	_____

Walking (3 mph)	_____	× 10	_____
Golf	_____	× 6	_____
Softball	_____	× 6	_____
Total Score			_____

A score of 100 is excellent. A score of 60 is good. A score of 40 is fair. A score of 20 or less indicates a need for more exercise.

8 / Keep Happy

Author Lee Neville tells of the older woman he discovered playing hopscotch with her little granddaughter. Greatly intrigued, the writer stopped to observe the match. Not only did the senior citizen enjoy it but she displayed an amazing vigor for her age. The game over, the youngster clapped her hands and cried, "Grandma, I won! I won!"

The grandmother turned to Neville and said, "I haven't had such fun since I tried my grandson's skateboard. My daughter keeps telling me, 'Act your age, Mom!' But I keep answering, 'I'll be any age I choose. Nursing homes are filled with old ladies acting their age!' "

Samuel Taylor Coleridge described what he meant by the happiness of life, made up of many fragments of time—"the little soon-forgotten charities of a kiss or a smile, the joyous games, a kind look, a heartfelt compliment and countless pleasurable feelings."

The Apostle Peter writes to Christians, "Even now you are happy with the inexpressible joy that comes from heaven itself" (1 Pet. 1:8, TLB).

Happiness includes the expectation of great hopes to be pursued and realized. Happiness comes from many things: exerting an effort, having meaningful goals, enjoying exotic aromas, having exciting experiences, viewing beautiful sunsets, studying new subjects, loving good friends and family, and—most important—immersing oneself in the presence of God.

"This is the source of the joy of adventure," says Tournier, "the joy of doing good for something and for someone—for God who has called us to do it for Him and for mankind."

1. *Keep laughing*

Our dear friend Carlton Booth has remained for us a constant example of joyful living. The songwriter Homer Grimes has written a number of hymns for Dr. Booth and calls him "the finest example of refined spiritual exuberance." His wife, Ruth, to whom Carlton has been married for fifty-two years, says, "He loves a good story and shows a keen sense of humor whether he is telling it or listening to it." And she adds, "He even laughs in his sleep when dreaming and remembers the details the next morning!"

The book of Proverbs says, "A cheerful heart does good like medicine." Exercising our good emotions is a major factor in the buildup of our physical chemistry.

A dramatic account of recovery from a deadly disease is found in Norman Cousin's book *Anatomy of an Illness*. Doctors had told him he was suffering from a painful collagen illness—a disease of the connective tissues. Nodules had begun to appear on his body and at one point his jaws were almost totally locked. The doctors termed the disease "ankylosing spondylitis" and assured him he had only one chance in five hundred. One physician told him that he had never witnessed a single recovery from this ailment.

Commenting on this gloomy prognosis, Cousins said, "It all began when I decided that some experts don't really know enough to make a pronouncement of doom on a human being. I hoped they would be careful about what they said to others. They might be believed and that could be the beginning of the end."

In addition to a daily dose of twenty-five grams of vitamin C, Cousins began a program of daily laughter. He began with funny films shown on his own projector. Among them were "Candid Camera" and Marx Brothers' films. "I made the joyous discovery," he relates, "that ten minutes of genuine belly laughter had an anaesthetic effect and would give me two hours of pain-free sleep." He would repeat the procedure as needed. After each dose of laughter, sedimentation rate readings decreased at least five points. At the end of a week Cousins could move his thumbs without pain, and sedimentation registered at a rate of 80 (it had been 115) and was dropping rapidly. Some months later he was free of pain and able to return to his work at the *Saturday Review*.

Dr. Albert Schweitzer, commenting on such amazing recoveries, said: "Each patient carries his own doctor inside him. . . . We (physicians) are at our best when we give the doctor who resides within each patient a chance to go to work."

And laughter can be the Lord's hand on a troubled soul. One day during the most difficult time of the Civil War, President Lincoln convened his cabinet and told them that some serious business needed to be discussed. Looking at the anxious faces, he decided to lighten the moment by reading a hilarious portion from an Artemus Ward book. However, he soon noticed that the cabinet members were incensed at his "foolishness."

With a sigh, Lincoln laid aside the volume and said, "Gentlemen, why don't you laugh? With the fearful strain that is on me day and night I should die if I did not laugh occasionally. You need this medicine as much as I." Then turning, he drew a small white paper from his stove-pipe hat. It was his first draft of the Emancipation Proclamation.

Laughter is something we create ourselves; it sets us apart from the lower creatures. It grows out of a sense of the ridiculous and a realization that there is a great gap between the ideal and the real. It should be part of our reaction to life and of not taking ourselves too seriously. Someone has said that the lowest kind of laughter is that which laughs *at* others. The next highest is that which laughs *with* others. But the highest and best laughter belongs to the person who laughs at himself. When we can do that, our worries shrink inside us.

2. *Keep playing*

Some years ago Dr. Karl Menninger's clinic in Topeka conducted a study on the benefits of play. He reports some conclusions drawn from the inquiry in his book *Love Against Hate*: "People who don't play are dangerous. There seems to be a general idea that recreation is all right if one doesn't take it too seriously. My belief is that there should be a balance and that sometimes greater danger lies in not taking it seriously enough." He indicates that: (1) For some few adults, play can be an indulgence and still be helpful. (2) But for many, play is psychologically therapeutic and allows one to "visit" his happy childhood when responsibility did not hamper him. (3) For still others, play allows an adult to express aggressions in harmless ways not otherwise permissible.

To keep young, one must keep taking some risks, either physical or emotional. A childlike ability to hazard some slight risks in play can make a person young at seventy. Further studies indicate that taking these risks helps a person remain creative, attractive and energetic throughout a lifetime.

An older person riding a rubber raft down the Colorado with flushed cheeks and twinkling eyes is young. Games without at least some risk yield no exhilaration, especially when they become too routine. There are even non-sport risks like a Filipino bamboo dance I witnessed recently that brought vivacity to a group of touring seventy-year-olds. Or there was the party preparation at a retirement village that stirred the excitement of some eighty-year-olds.

If you can remember the last time you attempted a game that made you seem inept, silly or clumsy, you might gauge where you stand on the youth scale. Attempting something even a trifle daring (such as an unscheduled weekend away from home without notice) can add zing to living.

"Going away to a camp for older citizens," writes Victoria Irwin, "can make one feel like a kid again." The Buss Inn in Massachusetts is an example of a growing phenomenon that many church and civic groups are encouraging. Founded in 1970 as a retreat for young people, Buss Inn began to make room for at least sixteen folk over fifty-nine. Similar camps have sprung up elsewhere. At a camp in Santa Cruz, California, the Salvation Army hosts one-hundred-twenty older campers at a time. A ranch outside Seattle provides three-day trips for people over fifty-five. In Eureka, Missouri, the Kiwanis provide a camping facility for about one hundred seniors. Success has been so good that the service club is planning more such retreat centers.

These facilities often stimulate bored retirees to perk up and enjoy life once more. Mary Newton of Buss Inn reported one summer, "We have had a couple of people who were recluses back home. They just sat in their apartments and never came

out. Here they come alive. They say they will never lock themselves in again!"

These golden-age folk have enjoyed themselves so thoroughly
that they are returning to the camps year after year. They take
field trips and recall flowers and stars they haven't thought
about since scouting days. Many have grasped a softball bat or
tennis racquet for the first time in forty years.

A recent survey by Research and Forecasters of New York
profiled the recreational habits of grandfathers up to age ninety-
three. The study found that forty-two percent play table games
and visit family and friends regularly. Sixty-five percent love
traveling as a leisure activity. Seventy-three percent include
walking in their daily regimen while twenty-five percent engage
in regular swimming. Bicycling is enjoyed by twenty-two percent, calisthenics by eighteen percent, and bowling by seventeen
percent. Golf occupies fifteen percent.

The director of the survey concluded, "The life expectancy
for males is seventy-four years of age for those who have lived
past sixty. It is therefore reasonable to assume that a substantial
number of today's youthful, spirited, fully-involved grandfathers
will become great-grandfathers. Their affirmative views about
family, work, and life represent a strong sign of hope for the future."

3. *Keep up with hobbies*

One's retirement may often seem like an amputation. It is
likely that you will have invested thirty or forty years of emotional commitment into your job. Now you will probably want to
reinvest your sense of commitment as quickly as possible to avoid
frustration or emptiness. After a job has ended, one's creative
needs may leave one feeling incomplete or dissatisfied for a time.
Here is where hobbies can fill a great void.

Frank Medina of California collects windmills for his hobby.
A seventy-three-year-old retired farmer, he enjoys an avocation
that he has loved for over sixty years. "I have been nuts about
windmills since I was a kid," he says. "I love to hear them go
'round. I love to sit and watch them spin."

Frank refers to himself as "King of the Windmills," and as proof he has erected more than one hundred of them in his front yard. He has spent over fifty thousand dollars on them thus far but keeps advertising for more. His fame, according to Charles Hillinger in the *Los Angeles Times*, has spread across the country and sightseers drive past regularly to view his display. It is evident that this recognition and sense of adventure give meaning to Frank's retirement days. "People drive by my place," he says, "and can't believe their eyes." He keeps track of each windmill's age and condition and finds that most of them were built in the 1920s and 1930s. The oldest, however, dates back one hundred seven years.

The windmills are not in the greatest condition, Frank concedes. Some are rusted and bent with much use. None is under forty years of age, but each has a well-used look. Of the one hundred-odd windmills in the front yard, practically all have one or more birds' nests. "I hope to fill my twenty acres with at least two thousand windmills before I die," Frank says.

According to Paul Tournier, "The retired worker will find that his leisure activities need to be something more than aimless diversions. They will have to be of a quality that will give meaning to his life." In pre-retirement days we may find certain activities and hobbies enjoyable for a short time. But later we may discover that they do not stand the test of time. They may lose their attractiveness when they do not meet continuing needs.

"The things that count," continues Tournier, "are the things we do freely . . . all those things that widen our social relationships, everything that diversifies our lives. . . . What matters in leisure is that it should be leisure 're-creation' in the true sense of the word, an exciting pleasure." Such hobbies keep one youthful in outlook, active, vigorous, enterprising and eager to learn.

Sometimes a sideline may become so beloved that it can develop into a lifelong vocation. This is true of Dr. Louis Camuti who has loved pets all through his sixty-year career as a veterinarian. He began to focus especially on cats in mid-career, developing a strong love for them. "A cat is less demanding than a dog," he observes, "but it's a greater challenge." Hence he became a cat specialist.

Throughout his eighty-seven years, writes Terry Kirkpatrick for the Associated Press, Dr. Camuti has cared for many kinds of animals, from ocelots to pigeons and honey-bears. But in his autobiography he tells how in his fifties he began to make house calls, especially on sick cats. Since his invalids invariably fled his hypodermic needles, he titled his book, *All My Patients Are Under the Bed*.

He regards his service to cats as a genuine calling. "I have a road to travel," he says of his drive to help felines, for he sees beyond the cats themselves. He believes that he helps the cat owners in their quest for social expression. "There are a lot of lonesome people in this city," he states. "They've got to love something. . . . A cat eases their tensions when they're tired and alone. If I ignore the animal, I do some harm to the person."

Many hobbies or leisure-time activities will not match Dr. Camuti's occupation, but can be just as satisfying. There may be some that are merely diversions, such as checkers, chess or Monopoly, but they pass time pleasantly and encourage warm social contact. Many people will want creative outlets such as writing, painting, woodwork or cooking. These permit the person to create to the extent he or she may wish and yet conclude with prideful products. Other folk love hobbies that can bring status or recognition. But as Christians, we should look to the basic end, that it will result in glory to God.

Jean Domenach says of leisure: "There is something 'sacred' about it. It is the part of our lives which must not be spoiled by mere routine work; it allows us to have a contact with nature and others which is both friendly and poetic, rather than just utilitarian."

4. *Happiness is . . .*

The Apostle Peter, in his first letter to the scattered Christians, indicates that happiness is a Christ-generated experience: "You love him even though you have never seen him; though not seeing him, you trust him; and even now *you are happy* with the inexpressible joy that comes from heaven itself" (1 Pet. 1:8, TLB—emphasis mine).

Allen Gardiner, the martyr missionary to Tierra del Fuego, understood this God-motivated happiness under dreadful circumstances. After his companion was killed by unfriendly natives and he himself was starving to death, Gardiner retreated to his small boat for refuge. Rescuers found a note beside his body with these words: "My little boat is a Bethel to my soul. Asleep or awake I am happier than tongue can tell. I am starving, yet I feel neither hunger nor thirst. I feed on hidden manna and drink at the King's well. I am not disappointed, for I remember that one soweth and another reapeth."

In a study by Dr. Jonathan Freedman, professor of psychology at Columbia University, it was established that older people make up the happiest sector of the population. "Why should the oldest group have more people who are very happy than any other age group?" he asks.

He observes that apparently happiness does increase with age. Evidently, older folk have learned the lesson of *acceptance*. "Satisfaction," he comments, "is a big step toward happiness." Another factor seems to be *optimism*: "Almost eighty percent of older women say they are optimistic compared to only sixty-five percent of younger groups." This apparently emerges from a sense of inner satisfaction: "Most of the important decisions (in life) have been made; whatever accomplishments, relationships, successes, recognitions, loves, and so on, that are going to be yours have already occurred." In general, golden-age people say, "Whatever I did, I did it and it wasn't too bad; I am more or less satisfied with it, and I am pretty satisified with my life now."

Faith, of course, plays the most important role in the life of the older Christian. "If your values are correct, if your life has meaning, you are more likely to be happy," reports the survey. Although moments of *great* excitement are probably fewer for older folk, this is compensated by other more quiet types of satisfaction. Those in tune with God and His creation enjoy life more than those that are not. "Their health is better," says the study, "and they report less anxiety, tiredness and loneliness." They are also reported as being in good shape psychologically.

Ernest Dichter, who has also done motivational research on life-satisfaction, says, "Happiness is a positive state of affairs. It is your reaction to your whole life. But it can be broken down and analyzed. It is an emotion of the heart, a zest for living; but it is expressed in such concrete everyday experiences as perhaps baking a chocolate cake."

Dichter then describes the necessary inwardness of the happy person: "(Happiness) is something you can work out for yourself, and it is important that you do so. Without the happy adjustment, you are unlikely to find material success and you are certain not to find *living* success."

The best advice on happiness comes from the Lord himself: "Happy are those who long to be just and good, for they shall be completely satisfied. Happy are the kind and merciful, for they shall be shown mercy. Happy are those whose hearts are pure, for they shall see God. Happy are those who strive for peace—they shall be called the sons of God" (Matt. 5:6-9, TLB).

Most importantly, no person can be truly happy who does not love others. The following pages will seek to examine this vital aspect of life.

PERSONAL HAPPINESS EVALUATION

Before moving on to the chapter on loving, you may want to evaluate your happiness quotient:

I. Answer yes or no to the following: Yes   No

   1. Do you like almost everyone you meet?   _____ _____

   2. Can you fit in with almost everyone?   _____ _____

   3. Do you like to help the very young, the very old, or the very needy?   _____ _____

   4, Do you have little free time?   _____ _____

   5. Do you have several close friends (2 to 4)?   _____ _____

   6. Is your time busy and useful?   _____ _____

   7. Are you mostly confident and unworried?   _____ _____

   8. Are you an "easy to please" patient when you are sick?   _____ _____

   9. Can you stand being contradicted and keep smiling?   _____ _____

  10. Can you change your plans fairly quickly without getting too upset?   _____ _____

  11. Can you say no to a new request when you are already overburdened?   _____ _____

  12. Can you feel pleased when a friend gets ahead of you in a job promotion or in a game?   _____ _____

  13. Do you have someone special whom you love and who loves you?   _____ _____

  14. Do you pray and read your Bible regularly?   _____ _____

  15. Can you forgive a hurt and get over a grudge fairly easily?   _____ _____

  16. Do you feel there is an important reason for living?   _____ _____

  17. Do you believe these are the best years of your life?   _____ _____

  18. Do you rarely feel miserable?   _____ _____

19. Can you adapt to change fairly quickly? _____ _____
20. Do you feel you can trust most people? _____ _____

Totals _____ _____

(In totalling your score, count 5 for each "yes." A total of 65 or more means your happiness quotient is good. 45 to 65 is fair. Under 45 is poor.)

II. As a follow-up on specific goals, this next test is designed for you to zero in on tangible happiness (or unhappiness) objectives:

	Yes	Some	No
1. Do you want to be well-recognized in your area?	_____	_____	_____
2. Do you wish to work for human betterment?	_____	_____	_____
3. Do you feel it is important to earn a lot of money in the process?	_____	_____	_____
4. Do you feel you are part of a meaningful group that is useful?	_____	_____	_____
5. Would you like to have a prestigious title?	_____	_____	_____
6. Do you look forward to each day and to the future with anticipation?	_____	_____	_____
7. Do you want to be a part of a well-known organization?	_____	_____	_____
8. Do you sense God's watchcare over you most of the time?	_____	_____	_____
9. Do you feel you are absolutely necessary to your job and no one can do it as well as you?	_____	_____	_____
10. Do you feel that you can meet most days successfully?	_____	_____	_____
Totals	_____	_____	_____

Score 3 for every "yes" on even-numbered questions
Score −3 for every "yes" on odd-numbered questions
Score 1 for every question answered "some"
Score −3 for every "no" on even-numbered questions
Score 3 for every "no" on odd-numbered questions

A perfect happiness score is 30; a fair happiness score is 20-25;a moderate happiness score is 10-15.

III. Abigail Van Buren quotes an anonymous prayer which you may wish to use to evaluate your daily activities that can lead to wholeness and happiness. Check your acceptance of each fact:

	Yes	No
Lord, you know better than I know myself that I am growing older and will someday be old.	_____	_____
Keep me from getting talkative and particularly from the fatal habit of thinking I must say something on every occasion.	_____	_____
Release me from craving to try to straighten out everybody's affair.	_____	_____
Keep my mind free from recital of endless details—give me wings to get to the point.	_____	_____
Give me grace enough to listen to the tales of others' pains. Help me to endure them with patience.	_____	_____
Seal my lips on my own aches and pains—they are increasing and my love of rehearsing them is becoming sweeter as the years go by.	_____	_____
Teach me the glorious lesson that occasionally it is possible that I may be mistaken.	_____	_____

Keep me reasonably sweet; I do not want to be a pseudo-saint (of course, all Christians are saints

in the theological sense)—some saints are hard
to live with—but a sour old person is one of the
crowning works of the devil.   _____ _____

Make me thoughtful, but not moody.   _____ _____

Make me helpful, but not bossy.   _____ _____

With my vast store of wisdom, it seems a pity
not to use it all; but you know, Lord, that I want
a few friends at the end.   _____ _____

9 / Keep Loving

A seventy-five-year-old man recently went to the doctor for his regular checkup. "You're in great shape," said the physician. "What have you been doing by way of exercise or special diet?"

The man smiled and said, "When we were married fifty years ago, my wife and I agreed on a set of rules. She promised that whenever I got angry she would never answer back. And I promised that whenever she got angry I would take a long walk. As a result, for the last fifty years, I have lived pretty much of an outdoor life."

"The path of love is not always smooth," goes an ancient saying, whether it be love for spouse, family, friends, or country. If love between two persons involves deep exchanges, the result will be deep mutuality. When a person really gives oneself, he or she can charge the loved one with a psychic vigor which energizes and nourishes. When expressed sexually for a spouse, it results in a mutual and very basic exchange of energy. Love brings the caring, understanding and encouraging that actually changes involved people.

"Love," says Dr. Smiley Blanton, "is not an exterior accompaniment of life, but the very stuff out of which life is fashioned."

There were only a few women who went down with the Titanic when it sank in 1912, but among the few was Mrs. Isador Straus. Throughout the panic of loading women and children into the lifeboats, she worked shoulder to shoulder with her husband to see that the helpless were secure. When all were safely overboard, Isador urged her to join the last lifeboat. Reluctantly, she took her seat and waited with the others to be lowered into the ocean. At the last minute, however, she sprang back onto the deck before Mr. Straus could stop her. Putting her arm into his, she snuggled closely and said, "We have been together through a great many years. We are old now. Where you go, I will go."

The best definition of love was written 2000 years ago: "If you love someone you will be loyal to him no matter what the cost. You will always believe in him, always expect the best of him and always stand your ground in defending him" (1 Cor. 13:7, TLB).

The most sacred human love-relationship belongs to man and wife. Indeed, it is so sacred that Scripture uses it as a symbol of Christ and His Church.

1. *Keep loving your mate*

There is a great joy, a great mystery about the union between two persons in marriage. If this union is strong, each of the partners has learned through the years to be more supportive and caring . . . and more intrigued by the other.

Anne Philippe, in her book *No Longer Than a Sigh*, expresses it beautifully: "I look at you asleep and the world you are in, the little smile in the corner of your lips, the flicker of your eyelids, your relaxed body, all these are mysteries. . . . We talk: your voice, your thought, the words you use are the most familiar in the world. We can even finish the sentences begun by the other. And yet you are, and we are, a mystery." Paul speaks of this mystery-relationship between husband and wife.

Such a relationship continues to reach through the years even after one of the partners may be gone. So close has the couple become that the thoughts of one have become fused with the thoughts of the other. As Genesis puts it: "A man . . . is joined to his wife in such a way that the two become one person" (Gen. 2:24, TLB).

Molly Picon, beloved folk actress and singer, lost her husband when she was eighty, after fifty-seven years of marriage. They had become so united that she was devastated for three months after his death. "I sat there and tore up bits of paper trying to find myself." Finally, she appealed to her agent and he was able to arrange an engagement for her at Carnegie Hall. "I got my songs and my act together," she says, "but my heart wasn't in it. I felt empty." Only by remembering one of his sayings was she heartened to go on: "It's no trick," he had told her, "to drink out of a full bottle. But it *is* a trick to drink from an empty one." His goal in life is one they had jointly evolved: "If I add something to my times, then that is my prize!"

Married love consists not only of physical attraction, but of shared interests, games, vocations and pastimes. The interests themselves can be absorbing. But beyond that, the give-and-take enriches the melding process between partners.

"How beautiful," says Tournier, "how grand and liberating this experience is when couples learn so to help each other. . . . No one can develop freely in this world and find full life without feeling understood by at least one person."

Our friend Marcie recently told of an unmarried cousin who had reached her mid-fifties without feeling completely fulfilled. One day, after reading an aviation magazine, she determined to learn to fly a plane. Some months later, delighted with the ease of acquiring this new skill, she set a new goal to fly a balloon. Hearing of her aeronautical interests, an acquaintance offered to teach her. Over the next few months she not only achieved her goal of balloon-flying, but she and her instructor fell in love and were married. Today this energetic couple travels widely in their own plane, sharing their many common interests.

Some fundamental ingredients in a happy marriage are so simple that they become profound. "People," says Professor Jonathan Freedman, "who are lucky enough to be happy with love, sex and marriage are more likely to be happy with life in general than any other folk." At first, this sounds trite, but it isn't. Love is mentioned more often than anything else as the one element missing from people's lives that, if supplied, would bring happiness. Even eighty percent of poor people do not mention money, but refer to love as critical to their happiness. Among those sixty-five and over, a survey finds that seventy-five percent regard married love as essential to a happy life. Love was to them not only a physical relationship, but one of shared interests, activities, values, family and friends.

One of the exciting stories of the Old West is that of Sara Plummer Lemmon, a botanist of the nineteenth century. In the year 1880, according to author Francis Morse, she and her husband John arrived in their new home, Tucson. Married in their middle forties, they plunged into their common love for the flora of Arizona.

In 1881, they set out to explore the Catalina mountains with their guide, E. O. Stratton. Sara was the first white woman to reach the highest peak in that range, and John was very proud. "We went to the highest peak of the Catalinas," Stratton recorded, "and christened it Mount Lemmon in honor of Mrs. Lemmon. . . . I chopped some bark off a great pine tree on the very top and we all carved our names." Sara is the only woman in United States history to have climbed a mountain named for her.

For the next quarter century, the two lovers gathered Arizona specimens and recorded them for posterity. It proved a hazardous life-journey for them. "This botanizing in the land of the Apaches," wrote John, "is a very risky business to be sure, but then its results are most satisfactory."

As they gathered plants, the Lemmons discovered many unnamed varieties. In her sixties, Sara identified a bloom of the daisy family that grows mainly in southeastern Arizona. It was a yellow flower somewhat similar to goldenrod, and John named it "Plummera," after Sara's maiden name.

To celebrate their silver wedding anniversary, John and Sara retraced their journey to Mount Lemmon in the Catalinas. Again guided by E. O. Stratton, they climbed on foot and mule to 9,157 feet above sea level. There, on Sara's mountain, they renewed their pledge of love to each other, Sara, seventy, and John, seventy-four.

After John's death in his eighties, Sara lived on in the warm glow of his devotion, active to the end. Among other achievements, she was responsible for California's adoption of the golden poppy as the state flower. In 1929, she died, full of years, love and accomplishment, at the age of ninety-three.

2. *Keep loving your family*

Ernest Burgess, authority on family life in the 40s and 50s, used to talk about "the companionship family." It involved the giving and receiving of love, equal responsibility for both parents, and reasonable democracy in decision-making according to each member's ability. As members grow and leave the nest, husband and wife must become re-acquainted while striving to maintain close ties with the increasingly extended family. Some households in the twentieth century have lost the ties between generations because of our emphasis on the nuclear family pattern.

Others, with all their weaknesses, exercise strong relationships with every member of the family no matter how old or how distant. The cement in the Joseph Kennedy family has always been Rose, the mother, a warm, matriarchal figure. Now past ninety, Rose Kennedy remains alert, strong and loving, and has been so from the start. A neighbor in Hyannisport has watched this family for years and makes the observation, "I still think it's important for families to sit down together. Rose has always kept her family very close to her and people don't do enough of that anymore." On her ninetieth birthday, the State of Massachusetts honored Mrs. Kennedy "as a moving force for the development of the family unit." For the most part, she has kept herself behind the scenes. But she continues to instill in her family a sense of social justice, public service, and the practice of her faith. "I have often felt," she says, "that if God were to take away all His blessings and leave me with one gift, I would ask for faith. For with faith in Him, in His goodness, mercy and love, and a belief in everlasting life, I feel we can suffer every kind of temporary deficit and still triumph."

As a result, her family has had an amazing impact on U.S. history. Only the Adams clan, President John Adams and family, seems to have surpassed the Kennedy record of one ambassador, three senators and a United States president. Yet Rose remains surprisingly humble. One of her daughters describes her as "an extremely grateful person who feels fortunate for all the things in her life."

Rose Kennedy has a philosophy of action for herself and her family: "I believe in keeping interested, growing and learning. Sedentary people are apt to have sluggish minds. A sluggish mind is apt to be reflected in flabbiness of body and in dullness of expression that invites no interest and gets none."

Love displays itself as an emotion when another's life is of deep concern to you. It is an alliance of devotion which takes joy in another, sacrificing or even suffering for that person.

Another Rose—Rose McKinney—has children who have been the recipients of this kind of love for over a half century. An eighty-four-year-old daughter of a former slave, Mrs. McKinney has supported all of her children through university and graduate schools. Although she herself had to drop out in the eighth grade, she says, "The Lord blessed me just the same."

God did indeed bless Rose McKinney, allowing five of her children to earn doctorates and all of her sons and daughters to enter professions. Among them are professors, clergymen, writers, business administrators and psychiatrists. Out of twenty-nine grandchildren, twenty have college degrees and the others are still studying. They are filled with love for her and high ambition for themselves. "The McKinneys aren't taking over the world," she assures her listeners; "they're just interested in getting an education. It's *in* them!"

But it is *in* them basically because it was first in Rose. "I wanted them to be useful men and women," she reminisces. "I would pray for them that when they got old enough they would all go to school and then to college." As each approached college age, all the others joined in to support him or her through at least four years.

Some became discouraged, but Rose remained firm. It was disheartening through the depressions of the 20s, 30s and 40s. One daughter said, "We didn't have clothing like everyone else." She felt they often played the game of catch-up. "Many times we'd register for school in September but not start until November because we spent two months picking cotton to buy clothes and groceries . . . but my mother said, 'No, you will not drop out of school.' "

One of the sons who used to earn $2.50 a day picking cotton is now Dean of Admissions at the University of California, Santa Barbara. And another testifies, "I can look back and see my mother always standing at the door. As we left each morning she would say, 'Do your best!' "

In Paul's definition of love (1 Cor. 13), the first characteristic he mentions is patience.

A young wife felt there was continual friction between her husband and herself. On a visit to a pastoral counselor, she was told, "You need a menagerie in your home!" Puzzled, she said, "We have a cat and a dog, but they don't help much." With a twinkle in his eye, the advisor replied, "No. You need two bears: Bear and Forbear."

3. *Keep loving your friends*

True friendship is the crucial point of life itself—whether it be inside or outside the family. It is more than an *experience* for us; it is a *relationship*.

In a sermon at First Congregational Church in Phoenix, Dr. Hugh Lee beautifully pointed this out by using pointed sarcasm: "When you grow old, don't bother to enlarge your circle of friends. Say to yourself that old friends are the best friends and that to get acquainted with and adjusted to new friends is too much of a bother. To guard against making new and perhaps younger friends, you might want to stay clear of clubs and churches and other associations of people."

There is real risk in being known by another person in true friendship. It hazards the deepest parts of your being to exposure. Some folk shrink from this as too great a price. Others plunge into friendship for the joy it brings in knowing and being known through flashes of fellowship.

One of the most precious experiences of my life took place in Colombia, South America. There at a mountain retreat, I was privileged to administer communion to several hundred believers. Through an interpreter (my Spanish was limited) I broke the loaf and expressed the simple biblical thought, "As we partake of this bread we are pledging eternal Christian friendship for each other." Unexpectedly we were swept by the Spirit into a fellowship that I have rarely experienced. Tears mingled with joy. Language barriers meant nothing. We were communing in a heavenly dimension, although singing in Spanish and English:

"Spirit, now melt and move
 All of our hearts with love;
 Breathe on us from above
 With old-time power."

It was similar to the experience expressed by Paul Tournier: "Suddenly I found myself trembling inwardly. . . . I felt as if I were confronted by something supernatural, something that overwhelmed me."

"The real You encounters me by grace," says Buber, "and I enter into a direct relationship with You. . . . The basic communion can only be spoken with one's whole being!"

As Christians we do not merely enjoy relationships. In the realest sense—we *are* relationships. Think back to the most exciting moments of your life and you will likely find they involved other persons. My greatest learning experiences were with a Mrs. Smith in the sixth grade. I learned in her class because I was energized by her vibrant spirit. "Our personalities," says Howard Clinebell, "are formed by the significant relationships of our childhood."

"As we live," observed David Lawrence," we are transmitters of life. And when we fail to transmit life, life fails to flow through us."

One of our dear friends at the beginning of our marriage was Dr. Arthur Fish. We were studying at seminary then and were desperately short of funds. Learning about our need, Arthur and his wife Polly shared their home and encouraged us until we were able to get part-time jobs. As we were leaving his home, I expressed our gratitude and asked, "Doc, how can we repay you for your kindness?" His reply made a lasting impression: "Repay me by helping the next Christian you see in need. That's what I have done."

4. *Keep loving your true self*

The true self is that inner person which has been redeemed by God. It is the same soul center to which the prodigal came after years in a far country. "And when he came to *himself*," narrated the Lord, "he said . . . I will arise and go to my father" (Luke 15:17, 18, KJV).

"If anyone, therefore, will not learn from Christ to love himself in the right way," taught Soren Kierkegaard, "then neither can he love his neighbor. . . . To love oneself in the right way and to love one's neighbor are absolutely analogous concepts and are at bottom one and the same." A confident view of oneself is a giant step toward self-knowledge. And to lovingly know one's brother is to know oneself, for we are all created by the same Creator out of the same fabric.

This is why Ashton Welch could write: "I want to be your friend because you gave me a part of myself I never saw before. . . . You also taught me that life's meaning becomes so much more beautiful when shared with someone who really cares."

To know oneself lovingly is for a Christian one major source of his highest potential. Through this insight he perceives the difference between himself and the world. And with it he can also see his own life more clearly, shuttling backward and forward so that he may plan from the past for a wiser tomorrow. Moreover, the loving perception of self gives one deep understanding with one's neighbor and the ability to communicate. This relationship with others is part of what we mean by the "image of God."

5. *Keep loving God*

Although we will deal with this topic at more length in Chapter 12, it is necessary to emphasize that love for our Lord is the source of all our other loves.

John Nelson, one of John Wesley's disciples, was incarcerated for his faith in a jail located beneath a slaughterhouse. In his journal, Nelson described the cell: "It stank worse than a pigsty because of the blood and filth that flowed into it from above. . . . But," he added, "my soul was so filled with the love of God that it was a paradise for me."

It was this same love that won Toyohiko Kagawa to Christ in 1903. As a young student, Kagawa lay sick in the city of Kobe when he heard a knock at his door. "Do not enter," he said to the visitor, Dr. C. A. Logan, "because I have a contagious disease." The missionary visitor nevertheless entered and said, "I have something more contagious than disease. I bring you the love of God."

"It is by loving and being loved," said George MacDonald, "that we can come nearest to the soul of another. For in love we rush home to the Father and the Son and the many brethren—rush inside that center of life-giving fire whose outer circles burn."

A loving relationship is the communion in which people commit themselves to one another's growth and healing. When I have a truly caring relationship with another, I seek to help him develop as a person. "Love flowers fully," says Clinebell, "only in a bond of mutual growth."

The much-quoted Roy Croft has expressed our love relationship so beautifully that I share some of his lines once again:

I love you not only for what you are,
But for what I am when I am with you.

. . . .

I love you for the part of me that you bring out.
I love you for putting your hand
Into my heaped-up heart and passing over
All the foolish weak things
That you can't help seeing there—
And for drawing into the light
All the beautiful belongings
That no one else had looked quite far enough to find.

Love takes time and shows itself in many experiences. It develops gradually through a multitude of contacts and interactions between persons. Love never lies idle to be picked up or put down according to momentary impulse. It flows in a continual exercise of care and selflessness. Not only is love a relation, but it is a creation.

Love leads inevitably to one necessary fruit—namely, service, the topic we will explore next.

Your love quotient might be measured, at least partially, by answering the following questionnaire:

I. With your husband or wife you may
want to gauge your compatibility.   Yes   Some   No

  1. Do you find many subjects hard to
     discuss?   ___   ___   ___

  2. Do you respect your mate's need for
     privacy?   ___   ___   ___

  3. Do you enjoy doing "your own thing"
     a lot?   ___   ___   ___

  4. Do you tell your dreams to your
     mate?   ___   ___   ___

  5. Do you ever criticize the other in
     public?   ___   ___   ___

  6. Do you share your thoughts and
     plans?   ___   ___   ___

  7. Do you often lose your temper with
     him/her?   ___   ___   ___

  8. Do you enjoy your mate's sense of
     humor?   ___   ___   ___

  9. Do you argue about money a great
     deal?   ___   ___   ___

 10. Do you share a fairly good sex life? ___   ___   ___

 11. Do you often wish your mate would
     discuss more things with you?   ___   ___   ___

 12. Do you enjoy looking at him/her
     often?   ___   ___   ___

 13. Do you often find yourself irritated by
     him/her?   ___   ___   ___

 14. Can you say "I love you" without
     prompting?   ___   ___   ___

144

15. Do you prefer being alone a lot? ___ ___ ___

16. Do you have similar tastes in most
    things? ___ ___ ___

17. Do you get angry at being criticized? ___ ___ ___

18. Do you enjoy church and spiritual
    things together? ___ ___ ___

19. Do you frequently interrupt each
    other? ___ ___ ___

20. Do you usually agree on spending
    decisions? ___ ___ ___

                              Totals ___ ___ ___

Score 5 for every "yes" on even-numbered questions
Score 5 for every "no" on odd-numbered questions
Score 2 for every "some"
Score −5 for every "no" on even-numbered questions
Score −5 for every "yes" on odd-numbered questions

A score of 100 is excellent; 75 is good; 50 is fair; with 40 or below,
you may need help.

II. Next you may want to check your friendship quotient:

                                              Yes   No

1. Do you often lose your temper when there
   is a disagreement? ___ ___

2. Do you try to explain your viewpoint
   calmly? ___ ___

3. Do you often feel misunderstood and
   unappreciated? ___ ___

4. Do you settle a difference on the spot? ___ ___

5. Do you remain angry for a number of days? ___ ___

6. Do you forget about a quarrel in a short
   time? ___ ___

7. Do you settle a problem superficially but stay hurt? ___ ___

8. Can you talk freely and easily with him/her? ___ ___

10. Do you have a trustworthy person who can advise you on personal and business matters? ___ ___

11. Do other people often annoy you? ___ ___

12. Do you enjoy visiting with some special person? ___ ___

13. Do you feel most people are basically selfish? ___ ___

14. Do you find most of your friends in church? ___ ___

15. Do you forget to keep your friendships in repair by writing, calling, visiting? ___ ___

16. Do you have someone who will defend or speak for you when the need arises? ___ ___

17. Do you keep most of your thoughts to yourself? ___ ___

18. Are you relaxed enough with someone to ask for help from him/her? ___ ___

19. Do you criticize your friend at once when you see him doing something you feel is wrong? ___ ___

20. Do you feel proud to be his/her friend? ___ ___

                                        Totals ___ ___

Score 3 for every "yes" on even-numbered questions
Score 3 for every "no" on odd-numbered questions
Score −3 for every "no" on even-numbered questions
Score −3 for every "yes" on odd-numbered questions

A score of 60 is tops; 45 is good; below 30 is poor and you may need counseling.

10 / Keep Serving

An unknown third-grader recently penned the definition of a grandmother: "Grandmothers don't have to do anything except be there. . . . Usually grandmothers are fat, but not too fat to tie your shoes. . . . Grandmothers don't have to be smart, only answer questions like, 'Why isn't God married?' Everybody should have a grandmother, especially if you don't have TV, because they are the only grown-ups who have time."

Maricopa County Hospital in Arizona has found a terriffic use for grandmothers who have time. Because the busy staff simply doesn't have the hours and minutes to share TLC with its ailing tots, mature women (and some men) have been recruited for its *Grandmothers' Club*. Miss Sally Carr, the recruiter, is looking for loving, caring folk to cuddle and rock about a dozen children in its pediatric division. Some of the youngsters are old enough to talk and enjoy having stories read to them—and other things that staffers are too busy to do.

"You don't have to sign up for the rest of your life," says Miss Carr. "Whether you can commit one hour a day, one day a week, or whatever, it's all important. But once you get here and feel so needed, you'll want to come back!"

The hospital has just a few basic requirements. Volunteers must have strong backs, possess good health, and be prepared to fall in love with the babies.

Dr. Karl Menninger designates this kind of service as one of the criteria for emotional survival—namely, the capacity to find satisfaction in giving rather than receiving. The psychiatrist also distinguishes other necessary qualities for continued health throughout life:
1) The capacity to love
2) The capacity to direct one's hostile energies into creative outlets
3) The capacity to relate to others with mutual helpfulness

147

These were the healing graces that saved Rev. and Mrs. David Lee of India from emotional breakdown at the turn of the century. Assigned to a mission station on the slopes of the Himalayas, their compound had been built on a treacherous mountainside. During one of the annual rains, both the missionary and his wife were preaching in the city of Darjeeling. While they were gone, their home was suddenly struck by a flash flood and landslide. They returned that afternoon, their splintered house strewn down the slope. With sorrowing hearts, they slowly retrieved the bodies of their six children.

Realizing the gravity of this blow, their mission board furloughed the Lees to Calcutta three hundred miles to the south. As they sadly nursed their grief, the couple began to notice many orphans living in the squalor of the city streets. One day, David Lee returned to the mission compound with a scrawny baby in his arms. "I think it is going to die," he told his wife. "I found it in the gutter." During the next week, the Lees poured all the love and devotion formerly reserved for their six lost youngsters upon this tiny infant. It began to gain weight, to grow and to smile. Soon after that another toddler was brought to the home, this time by Mrs. Lee. Then there were six, and then ten children depending on the missionary and his wife.

Appealing to churches in America, the Lees soon received enough funds to buy their first dormitory in the heart of Calcutta. Today the couple have long since gone to their reward. But after three quarters of a century, thousands of needy youngsters have received loving care from the Lee Memorial Home.

1. Serve through living sacrifice

The central theme of our faith is that of sacrifice—from Genesis to Revelation. Yet it is not in the death of a victim that God takes pleasure, but in the offering of human living. "I plead with you," says the Apostle Paul to the Romans, "to give your bodies to God. Let them be a living sacrifice—which is your reasonable service" (Rom. 12:1, TLB, KJV).

We need to discontinue living for ourselves. We owe it to the Lord to serve Him in all we are and in all we perform. "Let your life be consumed in service," says L. P. Jacks. "Consume yourself valiantly, cheerfully, creatively, skillfully. Put all your intelligence into your self-consumption; put all your courage into it. Waste no thought asking whether you are happy. Ask for no guarantees. But you will not be miserable. Not a gleam of radiance the less shall fall on your life, but a hundred times more."

Ninety-six-year-old Louise McLeod still serves others for God, despite failing eyesight and hearing. This is not a new dedication; she started her serving career when she was fourteen. She found an avenue for giving herself in the Red Cross and passed out doughnuts to Teddy Roosevelt's Rough Riders while they were embarking for Cuba. Today she still gives her time to the San Francisco Red Cross and does not feel she is strange. "I'm just a member of the antique department," she says with a smile.

For eighty-two of her ninety-six years she has been producing a multitude of things for the poor and needy. Sewing baby clothes, crocheting afghans, rolling bandages, making robes and slippers have occupied her happy years of self-giving. She did take one furlough—a year in 1918—to sing to the troops during World War I. Then she returned joyfully to continue her life of selfless devotion. At age fifty-nine, she donated a gallon of her blood for the war effort and became Marin County's (CA) first "Gallon Club" member. Although sixty was the age limit for giving blood, she managed to donate one more gallon before the Red Cross called a halt to her generosity.

At eighty she lost her husband and moved into the Episcopal Home in San Francisco. Americans were fighting in Vietnam, so she organized the residents into a sewing team to make and fill bags of gifts for the servicemen's Christmases. Today, nearly blind, she sees mainly with her hands, yet continues her service of "helps." Her secret for happiness? "Giving is the greatest joy in the world," she says.

The itinerant preachers of frontier America knew sacrificial service to an even more rugged degree. With unflinching determination they faced jails, mobs, sickness and repeated drenchings in the open, day and night. They struggled through malaria-soaked swamps with their Bibles in their saddlepacks. Halford Luccock comments on these early heroes of the cross: "How did they ever stand it? The answer is that they didn't. They died under it. . . . Of six hundred seventy-two of those first preachers whose records we have in full, two-thirds died before they had been able to render twelve years of service!" Although the majority burned themselves out early in service to the Lord, some were like Freeborn Garretson, who left his journal to record his fifty years of service: "I traversed the mountains and valleys, frequently on foot with my knapsack on my back, guided by Indian paths in the wilderness. I often had to wade through morasses, half-leg deep in mud and water. Frequently I satisfied my hunger with a piece of bread and pork from my sack, quenching my thirst from a brook, and resting my weary limbs on the leaves of the trees. Thanks be to God! He compensated me for all my toil, for many precious souls were awakened and converted to God."

Reginald Heber, the great missionary who gave his life in India in 1826, wrote these words from his own service-oriented experience:

> A glorious band, the chosen few
> On whom the Spirit came,
> Twelve valiant saints their hope they knew
> And mocked the cross and flame;
> They met the tyrant's brandished steel,
> The lion's gory mane;
> They bowed their necks the stroke to feel.
> Who follows in their train?
>
> A noble army, men and boys,
> The matron and the maid
> Around the Savior's throne rejoice,
> In robes of light arrayed;
> They climbed the steep ascent of heaven
> Through peril, toil, and pain.
> O God, to us may grace be given
> To follow in their train.

2. Serve with a devoted heart

"I was feeling sorry for myself and spending all my time at it," admitted one woman recently. "My husband had died and all my children were grown and gone. I felt completely unwanted and forgotten. Then the phone rang. It was a long-lost friend whom I hadn't thought of in years.

" 'John and I were sitting here reminiscing and thinking of

you,' said the voice, 'and something told us to call you. How are you?'

"My eyes filled with tears and I could hardly get out the words of thanks. The glow of that phone call has stayed with me for weeks. What a thoughtful thing to do!"

Just a small gesture—to pick up the phone, to write a note, to make a visit, to bake a cake or to breathe a word of prayer or encouragement—but such a gesture can mean the difference between darkness and light. The open heart is not merely conforming to being "average." It is repaying indifference with love and returning giving for greed. The time to share our hearts is now, the place is here—for the sheer joy of God's goodness to us.

"I've seen much bread cast upon the waters," said Channing Pollock, "and it was returned to the giver all buttered, covered with jam, wrapped in wax paper and marked with love."

Lillian Dickson, director of the world-famous Mustard Seed, has poured her life into thousands of needy people over the past half-century. She started out serving from her own home while her beloved husband Jim was busy with his own mission work. Today in her seventies, she barely gives herself time to breathe, but God strengthens her every move. Jim is now with the Lord, but she has adopted a worldwide family. During thrice-annual speaking tours to churches in North America, she pleads with folk to share with her hungry children.

In a recent prayer letter, Lillian wrote from Taiwan: "Our work with the Lord is terribly interesting because it is with people in need of help. And no two days are the same. But now I must take the stairs more slowly still wondering what each day will bring forth." Her heart of compassion works overtime, usually active in several things at once.

"While writing this letter," she penned, "I felt someone near and looked up to see a pretty girl standing near my desk with a baby in her arms. It was the old, old story. She had been thrown out of her home and could not support the baby and herself, and would we take the baby? Of course we would."

Lillian gathers these loveless tots from many desperate places in Southeast Asia and finds homes for all. Her Mustard Seed helps a dozen or so orphanages, and couples from the Western world beat a path to her door. "We adopted out four infants from our Home last week," she said not long ago, "and it is so satisfying to put an unwanted baby into eager, loving arms of parents who will cherish it."

Her own arms of love reach out to countries from Taiwan to New Guinea with homes, schools, clinics, and conference centers.

Lovingkindness like hers is the inability to remain at ease when others are clearly not at ease, nor to remain wealthy when others are poor. Through her devoted heart the starvation in these countries is stirring hearts of church people to the gospel imperative, "Feed my sheep. . . ."

3. *Serve with imagination*

There are times when serving others takes some creative thinking. Christians often ask, "To whom should I give?" "When?" "How much?" "Where can I best serve?" One elderly man in Philadelphia had a brimming heart but a modest pocketbook. Because all his loved ones had died and he was alone in the world, no one was expecting a gift from him on a recent Christmas. So he started his shopping on Market Street by going from store to store as though his family were still alive. He priced presents for his mother and father, others for his brothers and sisters; but since they were all now dead, he didn't actually buy anything. He totaled up the imaginary bill and sent the equivalent in real cash to the neediest downtown mission he knew.

Unless people can share in such openness, they are, says the Lord, "like the chaff which the wind driveth" (Ps. 1:4, KJV). In South America there is a kind of plant that puts down its roots only for short intervals, long enough to build up its strength. But when the soil becomes dry, the plant draws itself up and blows away, searching for yet another moist area where it can sink temporary roots again. Its entire lifetime is spent rolling from one place to another until it eventually dies as a bundle of dry leaves and dead roots. Sadly, there are folk like this who drink only at others' springs, until they die—an unfulfilled bundle of thirst and desire. One can only become his truly healthy self by sharing nourishment and love with those nearby for the sake of Jesus. He learns the meaning of his life only by surrendering his ego in service for others.

Seventy-year-old William Norris heads a corporation dedicated to imaginative ideals called Control Data. It has built high technology plants for neglected central city areas. And it has invested in farming ventures for under-funded regions from the desert southwest to the Alaskan tundra.

Recently, Mr. Norris and his associates rediscovered a need with which the United States has been struggling for most of this century—namely, making small family farms profitable.

Thinking back to his own boyhood days on a small farm in Nebraska, Mr. Norris sympathizes with the creed "small is beautiful." Hence, Control Data has funded a community of small-sized farms in Princeton, Minnesota, that he terms "Rural Venture." It is building hoghouses, goose sheds, dairy barns and earth-sheltered homes. George and Tammy Walker are among the young participants who are working and benefiting from this project. The company is also providing a course on "How to Run Your Own Farm."

In addition, the corporation has gathered and computerized pertinent agricultural information for successful farming. A new computer sits in the closed-down pool hall in Princeton. Each farm owner can punch up his daily information for management analysis.

George Walker and his colleagues are asked to raise one kind of livestock and grow five to ten acres of feed for their animals. His wife Tammy says excitedly, "If this works, it could be important for the whole country, and other young people can do it too!" Of course, there are skeptics who feel that the small farm is a thing of the past. But they do not discourage William Norris, the septuagenarian leader of Control Data. "If people didn't scoff," he says, "I'd know immediately that I was on the wrong track." Our motto should be like William Norris'—not "live and let live," but "live and help to live."

4. *Serve to the end*

"Be faithful unto death," the Lord said to the believers at

Smyrna, "and I will give thee a crown of life" (Rev. 2:10, KJV).

Franz Liszt dazzled musical audiences throughout his long career with his piano playing and composition. His early activity was brilliant, but worldly. But the latter part of his life evidenced a clear Christian commitment and a deepening of his work. The greatest piano virtuoso of the 19th century, he was ordained in his fifties and his work then took on an increasingly Christian tenor. As part of his calling, he devoted much of his free time to training young pianists in their art. And in his seventy-fifth year, only two weeks before his death, he played one of his most brilliant recitals.

Loyalty to God and His service creates this kind of integrity in a Christian's life—and if we lose it, all is lost. Service drenches our life with meaning and flavor. Loving service cannot be produced on some sort of spiritual assembly line nor can it be blueprinted. The spontaneous source of godly service is the Christian heart aflame with love for its Lord out of which springs self-worth.

Although not a Christian, Marc Chagall is clearly in the Judaeo-Christian tradition and displays this same firmness. In his seventy-fourth year, he was commissioned to create twelve stained-glass windows for the chapel of a hospital in Jerusalem. At seventy-nine, he painted two glorious murals at Lincoln Center's Metropolitan Opera. When he was eighty-five, a biblical museum was dedicated in Nice, Italy, entirely devoted to his works. At ninety-two, he still faithfully produced works glorifying the scriptural teachings he learned as a boy in Russia.

Phyllis Bottome tells of a young lad whose father was being taken to a concentration camp during World War II. "But Father," asks the boy, "could they really kill you?" To this the father answers, "If they kill me, it could not help to spread their creed. It is those who kill who are weakened. . . . The ideas we stand for cannot be killed."

This was illuminated by the heroic martyrdom of Dietrich Bonhoeffer in Nazi Germany in 1945. Though young in age, he was a patriarch in faithfulness. "When Christ calls a man," he wrote at the end of his life, "He also bids him come and die. Faith is only real when there is obedience—never without it. Faith only becomes faith in the act of obedience."

Payne Best, one of Bonhoeffer's fellow prisoners at Schoenberg, wrote of him: "He was one of the very few men that I have ever met to whom God was real and close. On Sunday, April 8, 1945, Pastor Bonhoeffer held a little service and spoke to us in a manner which reached the hearts of all, finding just the right words to express the spirit of our imprisonment and the thoughts and resolutions which it brought. He had hardly finished his last prayer when the door opened and two evil-looking men in civilian clothes came in and said: 'Pastor Bonhoeffer, get ready to come with us.' Those words, 'Come with us,' for all prisoners had come to mean one thing only—the scaffold.

"We bade him good-bye—he drew me aside—'This is the end,' he said. 'For me it is the beginning of life.' "

The others remained to reminisce as he was taken away. One recalled that Bonhoeffer had often said, "The only fight which is lost is that which we give up."

One of his last prayers expressed his abiding faith in the midst of self-sacrifice:

Lord Jesus,
You were poor
And in distress, as captive and forsaken as I.
You know all men's troubles;
You remain with me
When all men fail me;
You remember me and seek me;
It is Your will that I should know You
And turn to You.
Lord, I hear Your call and follow;
Do, Lord, help me now.

Like millions of others, he was killed by order of Himmler as "an enemy of the state" (the Nazi officials referred to it as being "extinguished"). Eberhard Bethge, a fellow prisoner, said, "His ashes were thrown into the wind. There was no funeral, no sermon. And today there is no grave where reverence can make up for what was denied at the time of chaos." But, like Abel, "he being dead, yet speaketh" (Heb. 11:4, KJV).

As a person enters middle and "late adulthood," he sees his youth disappearing and fears it will be replaced by emptiness, lack of energy, lessening interests and vanishing resources. At this very time he needs to realize that all of life's potential is present and a new kind of integrity and wisdom can develop. A new path for creativity can grow out of his lifetime of stored resources. The final stage of our life can be one of godly nurturing for those that follow, who are still in their formative years.

Stephen Girard, one of America's most remarkable men, lived into his eighty-second year as a constant servant of others, while being at the same time one of our greatest financial wizards. In his latter years, he helped the United States finance the War of 1812, and after that founded the Second Bank of the United States. In his middle years he had given unselfishly of his personal energy and health to fight a yellow fever epidemic in the West Indies. Today, Girard College stands in the heart of Philadelphia, designated by his last will, for the care and education of poor children orphaned in that city. "When death comes for me," he wrote in his eightieth year, "it will find me serving unless I am asleep. If I thought I was going to die tomorrow, I should nevertheless plant a tree today."

Edward Everette Hale, a great poet and patriot of the 19th century, wrote his philosophy of service in a famous verse we used to memorize in school:

> Is there some desert or pathless sea
> Where Thou, good God of angels, wilt send me?
> Some oak for me to rend; some sod,
> Some rock for me to break;
> Some handful of His corn to take
> And scatter far afield,
> Till it, in turn, shall yield
> Its hundredfold
> Of grains of gold
> To feed the waiting children of my God?
> Show me the desert, Father, or the sea.
> Is it Thine enterprise? Great God, send me.

To continue to grow throughout life, we must serve Him and others to the end. But without a clear, vibrant vision, such service is not possible. Therefore, we will next explore some aspects of life-giving vision.

I. The following exercise may help you to assess your service quotient:

		Yes	No
1.	Do you often find yourself groping for meaningful jobs?	___	___
2.	Do you relate well to other people?	___	___
3.	Do you sometimes feel life is rather empty?	___	___
4.	Do you eagerly accept new experiences?	___	___
5.	Do you feel traditional patterns of service are always best?	___	___
6.	Do you like to find novel ways of helping others?	___	___
7.	Has it been a long time since you studied missions, wrote to missionaries or gave to missions?	___	___
8.	Do you often get involved in community work (e.g., hospitals, orphanages, civic service, etc.)?	___	___
9.	Was the best thing you ever purchased primarily for yourself?	___	___
10.	Do you tithe or give generously to church and/or missions?	___	___
11.	Has it been more than a year since you served on a voluntary committee of some sort?	___	___
12.	Are you a church or service committee officer (or have you been one in the past 3 years)?	___	___
13.	Would you prefer to give money rather than serve on a committee or work-group?	___	___
14.	Have you ever thought about serving short term for a missions organization, or Peace Corps, or doing other volunteer work?	___	___

158

15. Do you find it difficult to begin a service
    project for others?   ___ ___

16. Can you give up material possessions for job
    satisfaction?   ___ ___

17. Do obstacles frequently disturb you while
    serving on a committee or work-group?   ___ ___

18. Do you envision all of your work as some kind of
    ministry for others or God?   ___ ___

19. Do you sometimes omit sharing credit with
    others when your committee has been
    successful?   ___ ___

20. Do you listen more than talk when you find
    someone in need?   ___ ___

                                        Totals   ___ ___

Score 1 for every "yes" on even numbers
Score 1 for every "no" on odd numbers
Score −1 for every "no" on even numbers
Score −1 for every "yes" on odd numbers

A perfect score is 20 and your service quotient is excellent; a
good score is 15; a mediocre score is 10; with a score of less than
10, your service quotient may need sensitizing.

II. Next you may want to evaluate your service outlook on a five-
    point scale from poor to excellent (P=Poor; M=Moderate;
    F=Fair; G=Good; E=Excellent). Check the appropriate
    blanks.

    SERVICE QUALITY   P   M   F   G   E

1. Showing empathy (i.e., entering into
   another's feelings)   ___ ___ ___ ___ ___

2. Listening (i.e, hearing what the
   other's real needs are)   ___ ___ ___ ___ ___

3. Motivating (moving others into
action) ___ ___ ___ ___ ___

4. Mending and rebuilding (helping
especially with physical, emotional,
and spiritual needs) ___ ___ ___ ___ ___

5. Counseling (especially others who are
hurting) ___ ___ ___ ___ ___

6. Demonstrating the grace of
appreciation (willingness to share
credit) ___ ___ ___ ___ ___

7. Being supportive (when another
needs emotional props) ___ ___ ___ ___ ___

8. Encouraging another's self-esteem
(making someone feel good about
himself) ___ ___ ___ ___ ___

9. Demonstrating sensitivity to others ___ ___ ___ ___ ___

10. Giving praise for a job well done ___ ___ ___ ___ ___

11. Encouraging others to talk out their
problems ___ ___ ___ ___ ___

12. Refraining from judgment or blame-
giving ___ ___ ___ ___ ___

13. Surrounding another with warmth ___ ___ ___ ___ ___

14. Establishing rapport with another ___ ___ ___ ___ ___

15. Sensing another's need ___ ___ ___ ___ ___

If you have placed checks primarily in the G or E columns, your
service outlook is unquestionably high. Checks mainly in the P,
M or F boxes indicate a need for improvement.

11 / Keep Your Vision

A motto on a restaurant wall reads, "I used to dream about the salary I'm now starving on."

Our dreams and visions sometimes come true—only to be a disappointment. Others become all that we had hoped for and more. The late Bob Pierce, founder of World Vision, used to tell his co-workers, "Always give your dreams God-room!" The spiritual dimension of our forward look is essential.

Raphael's religious masterpieces grace many cathedrals and museums. He shared the same secret for success: "I simply dream dreams and see visions, and then I paint around those dreams and visions."

Spiritual sight allows us to see the unseen, to know the unknowable, and often to attain the impossible. It gives us the distant view of opportunity. Today there is so much in society that can discourage us. If a person uses the close-up view, he may rest in lethargy and imagine that things can never be any better. But when we receive the vision of God-possibility and see His force, we become winners for the Kingdom of God.

Peggy Ferriere, "the singing grandmother," is a changed person since she met Christ. "I hate the person I once was," she testifies. Although she once sang in night clubs, reports Dan Hall of the Associated Press, her aspirations are different now. At sixty-five, she had written at least sixty hymns since God turned her around. "I have the Lord now," she said, "and I'll travel."

Peggy's visions are centered in Christ. She recalls with pleasure the pastor who suggested, "Stop once a day and say to yourself three times, 'Jesus loves me, Jesus loves me, Jesus loves me.' Well, I've tried it and it works!"

She and her singing group, the "Jedidiahs," travel widely, fulfilling their vision of service. And it is all they could want. "The biggest nightmare for me," says Peggy, "would be to wake up and find things were different!"

1. *Keep a clear vision*

Once we have a vision, we must not let it become muddied. Visions have a tendency to blur and disappear. William James once remarked, "If you have a good emotion, do something with it. If you don't, you won't have it anymore."

David Burpee, in his mid-forties, had a clear idea in his mind of what he might do with flowers and particularly with marigolds. With only a few months of horticultural training, his dream became vivid concerning beautiful flowers. In fact, he grew so devoted to the marigold that he later lobbied (unfortunately without success) to have it declared the national flower.

"The only trouble with the marigold in the 1930s," he reminisced, "was that it smelled bad." Thus, he initially had trouble selling its seeds. Fortunately, a missionary friend in Tibet had found an odorless variety of the flower. Blending this with other types and experimenting endlessly, Burpee and his helpers encouraged a scentless bloom that now gilds America's gardens. Thereafter, his company developed countless varieties of other plants for an increasingly receptive world.

By following his vision, Burpee became an important bridge in the history of horticulture. *Flower and Garden* magazine described him as a "direct link in the history of American gardening. He brought his innovations to the people and made all available for a quarter a packet."

Johan Kepler sustained his clear vision despite contrary views by the rest of mankind at the time. From his studies, he perceived definite patterns in planetary paths. He deduced an elliptical path for each body in the solar system, and also reasoned a faster path for those closest to the sun. Though almost no one agreed with Kepler, he rested content with his vision. "Since God waited thousands of years for me to discover this truth about the stars," he philosophized, "I can afford to wait a century for someone to read about my discovery."

John Milton, blind and ailing in his latter sixties, refused to surrender his vision of *Paradise Lost* and *Paradise Regained*. In his closing years, he composed and dictated them to his devoted daughters. But the world could not see his vision of *Paradise Lost* and paid him a paltry ten pounds for the manuscript. It is clear that we need to pray for spiritual eyes as keen as Milton's so that we can see such vital visions.

Clear vision is marked by characteristics that can shake cobwebs from our minds:

1. We need a *focused* vision directed only toward essentials of our goal.

2. Our vision must not go so deeply into the problem that we become *burdened by unnecessary detail* and are kept from our objectives.

3. It should also be *unimpeded by unessential thoughts and acts* that could slow our progress.

4. Clear vision should be *illuminated by the indwelling Spirit* so that light can shine clearly within.

Helen Keller once said, "I have walked with people whose physical eyes are full of light, but who see nothing in wood or sky or sea, nothing in the city streets, nothing in books. Their souls voyage through the enchanted world with a barren stare. But it need not be so."

The Apostle Paul was able to say, "I was not disobedient unto the heavenly vision" (Acts 26:19, KJV).

Charles Fraas at eighty-two saw visions in trees, wrote Sam Negri in *The Arizona Republic*, that are hidden to most of us. Despite his age, every day he took two saws and a stepladder and walked into the oak and sycamore-lined canyons of southern Arizona. There he searched for burls that most people consider woodland cancers. Burls are abnormal growths that sometimes form where a tree has lost a branch and are generally considered unattractive. But Mr. Fraas envisioned a beautiful serving bowl in each.

Carefully he cut away those he liked best (some as big as footballs) and stowed them in his backpack. After collecting for the day, he returned to his workshop and commenced his loving labor. Using a variety of tools, he peeled away the bark until he reached the natural grain. Here God's nature has etched something very much like an intricate filigree. Turning the burl over, Charles created the inside of the bowl by removing the pulpy wood. With this rough work done, he began the refining process by sanding and polishing until his finished product gleamed.

"Lots of people can't see anything in these ugly chunks of wood," he ruminated, "but to me they're beautiful!"

An observer, on seeing work like Mr. Fraas', said, "A task without a vision is drudgery; a vision without a task is a dream; but a task with a vision is victory!"

2. *Keep an unselfish vision*

No person has given another person anything unless the gift has been costly to the giver. The more valuable it becomes, the better gift it will make. Whoever gives an unvalued thing to another has given nothing. This is what King David meant when he said, "I don't want to offer to the Lord my God offerings that have cost me nothing!" (2 Sam. 24:24, TLB).

Seventy-two-year-old Anne Elton learned not to make her pursuit merely a hobby while earning her college degree in gerontology. "I knew," she said, "that if I wanted to do something worthwhile, I had to develop a better background."

Today she works harder than ever before with an Atlanta group called Life Enrichment Services. As co-founder of the organization, she is helping senior citizens to help each other. Anne works full time without pay, organizing 1,000 senior citizens to serve 5,000 other elderly Atlantans. In the process, she has become an expert in her field and recently addressed a conference on aging as far away as Germany.

Mrs. Elton looks on this outreach as "the most satisfying of my life" and feels she is doing a better job than she did as a salaried executive in her younger years. Although it is hard work, she is unselfishly involved and feels at the height of her achievement. "After all," she says, "who knows more about the elderly than the elderly?"

It was such selfless vision that inspired David Livingstone when he read the words of Robert Moffatt: "From where I stand I can see the smoke of 10,000 villages that have never heard of Christ."

In tracing the Zambesi River to its source, Livingstone traveled 11,000 miles on foot through uncharted jungles. To spread God's Word, he suffered unbelievable dangers and hardships. Attacked by savage beasts and nearly killed, his dedication won the heart of the black man. He was fired to deep anger by the cruelty of the slave trade and became determined to crush what he called, "the open sore of the world."

In his latter years, Livingstone was racked by disease, attacked by wild animals, and often menaced by hostile tribes. Repeatedly he was robbed and abandoned by his own carriers, yet he marched on with his Bible. Henry Stanley reported that "not one man in a million would have pushed forward as he did." He pressed on until his body could go no farther. On May 1, 1893, he was found dead on his knees in a position of prayer, in a rude hut in the village of Ilala. He had been true to his heavenly vision to the end.

3. Keep an optimistic vision

"You will learn," said a successful grandfather, "that half the fun of life is having more possibilities than you can ever use!" But such opportunities do not come with their treasures on the outside. Each piece of "good fortune" must be torn open, mined and developed. Each day may present the opportunity of a lifetime. We must face every dawn with curiosity and courage that will bravely explore such openings.

Ted Dando of the APS Retirement Counseling Service says, "Retirement should not signal the end of an active, productive life. It can be the beginning of a new way of living that encompasses past experiences with a time to embark on fresh, new opportunities."

The Arizona Public Service offers a concentrated one-day seminar that effectively explains possibilities for the future for both retirees and pre-retirees. One sixty-five-year-old, commenting on this practical guidance, says, "The main thrust of the program is to present alternatives, to introduce things you normally wouldn't think of, and to put vague thoughts into focus. . . . There are expert speakers on every subject giving firsthand advice to individual situations."

Another lady of sixty-three had been preparing for retirement for fifteen years: "My mind just buzzed with ideas," she said. "It confirmed that the financial plans I have made through the years were correct. I was surprised more people hadn't made similar plans. Having done so, and knowing it, is comforting."

Then in an adventurous tone, she listed some of her plans: "I intend to paint the patio furniture, do macrame, spend more time with my friends and take advantage of daytime classes." And this was only the beginning of her catalog: "Later on I'd like to do volunteer work for the Arthritis Foundation. My new freedom may help fulfill my dream of selling my pencil sketches. I'd like to be part of one of the art shows in shopping malls and sketch people on the spot."

Very few of the world's great treasures of music, art or architecture have sprouted from ideal circumstances. The majority of them have blossomed in adverse conditions, such as poverty, pain, struggle, or advanced age.

At eighty, the beloved actress Helen Hayes remembered many happy, but also many adverse, circumstances. "I have learned," she said, "that I can meet the setbacks of life with grace." She felt that is what her faith has taught her. As she thought back, Miss Hayes seemed to find strength and creativity in some of the difficult circumstances she has experienced. "I have loved a lot in my life, which is not to say that a lot of things don't happen in everyone's life that cannot be controlled, and that also bring pain. A child dies . . . someone loved dearly dies . . ."

Somehow this all seems to have added beauty to her art and vision of the future: "There is a great discipline in the theater; and learning that discipline, absorbing it, accepting it, strengthened me to walk straight through life."

In her ninth decade, Helen sees visions and new horizons. "I am turning over a new leaf at eighty. I am about to launch myself on a career that does not draw limelight or too much public notice." She accepted an invitation to serve on the Advisory Committee to the White House on Aging. Concerning this and other tasks, such as her acting, she said, "You have to give of yourself; you have to work; you have to try, try, try every day and do better than you did the day before."

Miss Hayes has her periodic discouragements, but she will not allow them to get her down: "I know that I won't give up trying until I am at least a hundred!"

4. *Keep a simplified vision*

We need often to streamline our own vision in order to discover more creative living. Such a vision can motivate our living for years to come, while unbridled dreams can leave our life in disarray. We should shorten and simplify the limits of our insight.

The late Buckminster Fuller has been called "the first poet of technology." He designed his geodesic domes by analyzing nature's molecular structure and duplicating it in his drafting genius. To his death at eighty-eight, he still solved many intricate problems through such simplified visionary insight, basing much of his design on extensions of the isosceles triangle. During his earlier productive years, he conceived the Dymaxion car, constructed with an aircraft fuselage and a steering radius of only a few feet. Following this was his Dymaxion bathroom, stamping out the whole chamber just as an automobile body is formed.

Fuller's Dymaxion House (the word was derived from "dynamic" and "maximum") preceded the geodesic home and was a many-sided dwelling hung by cables from a central mast.

When he was a young man, Fuller survived a suicide attempt in Lake Michigan. Apparently this caused a kind of humanistic conversion experience and his subsequent decision to live: "You do not have the right to eliminate yourself. You do not belong to you. You belong to the universe." And following that episode in his life, he declared, "Everything from that time on has been done for the social benefit of all humanity."

Fuller's geodesic dome was perfected when he was in his sixties and has had a revolutionary effect on world architecture. African natives learned from him to make their huts in this many-sided form. And the U.S. Air Force followed his design for shelters along the D.E.W. Line. Structural experts have declared the geodesic pattern to be as self-sufficient as a butterfly's wing and as strong as an eggshell. It resists both winds and violent earthquakes. Its shape is found commonly in nature in the eyes of a fly, the cornea of the human eye, and the form of germinal viruses. According to reliable records, more than 200,000 of his geodesic domes were in use in 1983.

Fuller, at eighty-five, served as Professor Emeritus and lecturer at both the University of Southern Illinois and at the University of Pennsylvania. Although his vision was not from the perspective of an evangelical Christian, Buckminster Fuller's vision was simple and concise; he felt that mankind was still 2,000 years behind God's designs that are to be found in the earth, sea, and sky.

One is reminded of Jesus' words, "If therefore thine eye be single [the Greek word here is *haplous*, meaning simple or unified], thy whole body shall be full of light" (Matt. 6:22, KJV). Our Lord's concept seems to be that of folding our thoughts around one single insight in order to attain our clearest vision.

"I see with engineering," said Fuller, "how we can do so much with so little. I see a design revolution possible that could take care of all the people. . . . I got deeply involved in mathematics and came to the discovery of domes that could enclose space without any interior support."

Did his clear and simplified vision diminish over the years? "No," he related, "at eighty-five I could not be more thoroughly convinced that we have the options. I am hopeful we will find a young world and be eager to find a way to make it work."

5. *Keep a bright vision*

As one advances in years, he finds that it pays to have ever higher expectancies for the brighter side of life. Too many folk expect (and consequently receive) the worst. Even when things look blackest, it may not be the sign of a storm. It may merely be the shadow of God's hand. Rather than to worry, it would be far better to expect the sun to break through! Spirit-induced optimism creates a contagious force for good.

A wonderful lady in the Southwest describes her idea of happiness: "A rainbow after a short rain makes my spirits soar. The fantastic sunrises and sunsets turn my thoughts toward God and His miracles. And just when I'm sad that one of my seven rose bushes looks like it's dying, it brings forth a gorgeous, fragrant rose!"

A columnist adds this optimistic note: "What helps keep us all going is that just when we're most depressed, God and people surprise us with something wonderful."

The late Korczak Ziolkowski, who died at the age of seventy-four, is another example of noble design and vision. For more than thirty years, he and his family have worked on the world's largest sculpture—a carving of the Sioux hero, Chief Crazy Horse. The statue's head alone will measure 87 feet—even larger than the heads at Mt. Rushmore. One arm of the Indian chief will measure 263 feet (long enough for 4,000 people to stand on). During his lifetime the sculptor blasted away almost seven million tons of solid granite at Thunderbird Mountain, and expected to blast another million before the rough work was done.

The artist's vision was born of a request by a spokesman for the Indian tribes: "We Sioux chiefs want you to carve a mountain for us so that the white man will know that the red man has great heroes too." Crazy Horse, the chief who defeated General Custer at Little Big Horn, gave his life for his people the following year. Ziolkowski studied his hero's life and stated his vision succinctly: "Crazy Horse was one of many great and patriotic heroes, but his tenacity of purpose, his modest life, his unfailing courage and his tragic death set him apart from and above the others."

Although much of the carving still needed funding, Korczak was not discouraged. His family worked faithfully by his side and shared his vision. His son Joel said, "My brothers and I will finish the mountain if he dies. But he isn't going to die before it is done. [Unfortunately, he did die before completion.] If it takes until his ninetieth birthday, knowing my father, he'll be up there blasting the eastern face off the mountain." The sculptor was totally devoted to his dream. He had fallen a number of times, had broken several bones and cracked his spine. Despite that, plus arthritis and two heart attacks, he carved away.

Charles Hillinger, writing about Ziolkowski for the *Los Angeles Times*, said, "The man is as tough as the granite he sculpts. He is on the mountain every day from dawn to dusk. He will probably live to see his vision fulfilled."

Two famous authors, Daniel and Ruth (Frankel) Boorstin, have been proving the joys of upbeat vision for the past forty years. Together, they have written sixteen successful books. Their works have evolved from what they term "those old corny concepts of trust, love, support, and mutual respect." Most importantly, they believe those virtues are something to be excited about.

The birth of their third son created such enthusiasm in Mr. Boorstin that it prompted a nurse's curiosity: "Dan was so excited," reminisces Mrs. Boorstin, "that the nurse asked him if it was his first child. He said, 'No, it's my third.' Then the nurse decided it must be his first son. He said no, it was his third boy, but wasn't it exciting?"

Deborah Churchman, a news reporter, comments, "That seems to sum up the Boorstin attitude on marriage and on life." Certainly it is their view on writing, their mutual profession. It was particularly important during Daniel's three-volume work, *The Americans*, to have "someone there who understood, who could talk about the project, get excited about it and share the new insights as they came along."

Sharing a mutual vision has always been important to this creative couple: "You have to lead almost a double life," observes Mrs. Boorstin, "and see things not only from your own point of view, but the other person's too. If a woman is an immaculate housekeeper . . . and spends all day scrubbing and dusting and polishing, she should ask herself if this is what her husband really wants—a clean house and an exhausted wife?"

Summing up her philosophy and vision, she comments, "I have always been proud of my dust. It shows that I had something better to do. . . . We concentrated on the fun things of life—books and ideas."

Shrewd interpersonal dealings do not produce this kind of vision; it flows from illuminated insight. Not derived from possessions, neither can it be destroyed by a lack of them.

"Rise up, O believer," says Charles H. Spurgeon. "Cast away your sloth, your lethargy, your coldness, or whatever interferes with your love of God. Make Him the source, the center, and the circumference of all your soul's range. Be no longer satisfied with your dwarfish attainment. Aspire to a higher, nobler, and fuller life!"

"He shall give thee the desires of thine heart" (Ps. 37:4, KJV). The very highest longings that are in your mind (if we are delighting in Him and in His Word) have been placed there by His hand.

Jay Stocking, in the last century, found God the source of his vision:

O Carpenter of Nazareth, Builder of life divine,
Who shapest man to God's own law
Thyself the fair design,
Build us a tower of Christlike height
That we the land may view
And see like Thee our noblest work
Our Father's work to do.

O Thou who dost the vision send
And gives to each his task
And with the task sufficient strength
Show us Thy will, we ask.

It is with such an upward look that we shall next concern ourselves. Test your vision on the following two pages.

172

I. Testing your "vision" can be a highly subjective matter. But here are some leading questions that might help:

1. What event or person helped you initially catch your life vision and begin to set goals? Or was it a book, sermon or other motivator that set your eyes on this great vision?

2. Despite disappointments or setbacks, what kept you going toward this goal?

3. What step taken in your life do you most regret because it may have sidetracked you?

4. What milestones and persons along the way kept you going?

5. What experiences with the Lord do you feel redeemed you from failure?

6. What experiences have made you happiest because they helped you fulfill your dream?

8. What was the major discipline that kept you on track when you hit obstacles?

9. What was the greatest risk you ever took to fulfill your vision?

10. What do you consider to be the greatest sacrifice you have ever made for your goal?

II. A chart for sharpening your vision.

	Yes	Some	No
1. Are you enlarging your spiritual vision through reading and meditation?	___	___	___
2. Is your primary goal to serve the Lord Jesus Christ?	___	___	___

3. Are you learning new skills regularly that help toward your dream? ___ ___ ___

4. Are you learning to cope with change and disappointment as you work toward goals? ___ ___ ___

5. Are you reading new books regularly that increase the possibilities of fulfilling your vision? ___ ___ ___

6. Do you constantly find supportive material in the Bible that confirms your goal? ___ ___ ___

7. Do you cultivate friendships with people whose vision is similar to yours? ___ ___ ___

8. Do you feel you are learning the limits of your knowledge and the perimeters of your goals? ___ ___ ___

9. Have you set down your vision and goals in writing and do you review your progress constantly? ___ ___ ___

10. Do you pressure and gauge yourself against clear measurements of progress? ___ ___ ___

(If you can answer "yes" or "some" to all of these questions, you may feel you are on the road toward realizing your goals and dreams.)

12 / Keep Looking Up

A great deal of our inward unrest comes from basing our peace of mind on outward things. We spend too much time regretting failures, comparing possessions, longing for accomplishments or envying others. We think too much in terms of credits and honors, attainments and titles. We are continually attempting to score points.

Augustine, after his spectacular conversion in Milan, addressed his own soul and rebuked himself for confusing outer ecstasy with inner joy:

> Go back in your heart, you sinner, and cleave fast to Him that made you. Where are you going into rough places? Where are you going? Every good thing you have is from Him. But it is only good if you acknowledge that it *is* from Him.
>
> It is dangerous if you love any thing apart from Him who made it; and if you love the thing and forsake Him for it, you will find no peace where you are looking for it. Why do you insist on walking such difficult ways? You are seeking a blessed life in the land of death. It is not there. Our true life is in Him!

According to *Guideposts*, a young lady was studying voice at a New York conservatory recently. It meant sacrifice and hard work, and often going without meals. She was beginning to doubt whether this was God's will for her life. In a spirit of desperation one day, she picked up Albert Hay Malotte's *The Lord's Prayer* and began to sing those eternal words. It helped her so much that she sang it five or six times.

Several days later, she heard a rustle at the door and turned in time to see a note being slipped over the threshold. It read:

> Dear Neighbor:
> If you ever feel discouraged, perhaps this will strenghten you. Things had been going badly for me. So badly that I did not want to live anymore. But whenever I heard you singing, I cheered up a bit. You sounded like you had something to live for.

176

The other day I decided to end my life. I went into the kitchen and turned on the gas. It was then that I heard you singing *The Lord's Prayer*. Suddenly I realized what I was doing. I turned off the gas, opened the windows and drank in the fresh air. You sang the song six times, and you saved my life.

You gave me courage to make a decision I should have made long ago—to live for God. Now life is all I could hope. Thanks with all my heart.

Each of us must make this decision—to live for God. For only God can keep us looking up.

1. *Keep believing!*

The life of faith! What a wonderful experience it can be, and yet how comparatively few of us receive this life. It can lengthen our life and make it joyful. It can give pleasures we never could have known otherwise. And most important, it is life with Jesus who provides pardon for our sins.

A leading surgeon at Johns Hopkins said not long ago, "We don't know why it is that worriers die sooner than non-worriers. But it is a fact."

The book of Hebrews reminds us that faith means putting our full confidence in the things we hope for and being certain of things we cannot see. This faith is the only way the troubles of this world can be conquered.

A man named Theodore Booth related his experience of losing his son Bray in the airborne attacks of 1945: "God's existence never waned for me. He was still my Father. I knew His tears were as real as mine. I felt Christ beside me—my Shepherd and Lord. I knew He was suffering right next to me. I also knew that all tragic scenes are lighted by God's light and calmed by His love. And eventually I knew I could say with Job—and mean it: 'Though He slay me, yet will I trust Him.' "

Concerning this kind of reliance, Frank Laubach once stated: "Beware that your mind-set does not block the Lord. Open your soul wide, through which His healing power can flow." Alone in the dark times of our life, we often face our soul in all its weakness and loneliness. It is at that time we need God's Word and Holy Spirit to nerve and undergird us, putting steel into our spirits.

In a trench in Tunisia, after the battle of El Agheila, there was found the body of a soldier. In his hand was clenched this prayer he had written the night before:

Stay with me, God.
The night is dark;
The night is cold.
My little spark of courage dies.
The night is long;
Be with me, Lord, and
Make me strong.

Great riches await all Christians who grow older. One Christian told me, "For the person who has lived for the body, old age brings decay and disillusionment. But for the person who has lived for the spirit, it can be a triumph!"

Paul Tournier puts it: "To live with God is to share His everlastingness. He who has one foot in the infinite can accept his own finiteness."

To strengthen the Christian as years pass, he adds, "God has placed me here for my personal training. My real home is in heaven. And the more I have advanced in age, the more has earthly life seemed to me like an apprenticeship in the love and knowledge of God."

Like many pastors, I have seen many people open their hearts to Christ as Savior and Lord. But one of my most thrilling experiences was watching an older man commit his life to Jesus. I was then minister of a small church in the Blue Ridge Mountains of Virginia. The man had misspent his years in alcohol and other diversions. But one Sunday he wandered into our church with a desperate heart. My sermon was certainly not exceptional (since then I have examined its script many times). But an alliance of the Holy Spirit and the words I spoke brought this older person to God.

Thereafter his life was an amazing witness to God's grace. Gone were the alcoholism, the excesses and the immoralities. In their place for his remaining years, a glowing, reborn person witnessed steadily until he died.

Now is the time to start on the path of faith, if you have not already done so. Augustine voices a regret that we all entertain from time to time: "Too late I loved You, O beauty of ancient days, yet ever new! Too late I loved You. Behold You were within me, but I was abroad searching for You in vain things."

2. *Fulfillment*

A man once came to Jon McNeil, the successful urban pastor, saying, "I understand your church has a large debt, and I want to help." Leaving a blank check, he told McNeil to fill in the amount of money needed. McNeil notes, Underestimating the good will or ability of the stranger, I wrote in one-half the sum of the church's indebtedness." Some time later, the man returned and signed the check without looking at the figure. "I have always wanted to do something for God's work," he said. With some regret, the minister recalled his feelings. "I discovered that the stranger's heart was larger than my faith!" Too often this is the case in our relation to God. "We receive not because we ask not."

Perhaps we need some sort of continuing inventory of our lives, asking, "What am I doing with my hours and days? Do I merely get up and dress and eat breakfast? Do I wander off to my chores, sit at my desk for four hours and eat a hasty lunch? Does my life in any way reflect the joy of Christ? Do I routinely eat dinner, read the paper, yawn before the TV and fall into bed?"

In our self-analysis, we need to ask, "My hours—what are they leading to? Just saving a little money, enjoying an occasional vacation, eventually retiring, and then finally moving on to eternity?"

If we would only listen to what Christ has said to us: "As my Father hath sent me, even so send I you" (John 20:21, KJV). In actual fact, He has sent you and me to that breakfast table, that office, that kitchen, that school—to manifest His glory with our own personality as the channel.

If we can just realize this, we can be done with all the dullness and tedium of life. We are not only performing our best for home or school or business or even sports. We are doing our best for Him! Daily we are responding to His voice. If we have repented, we have been commissioned by God, and His glory surrounds us whether we see it or not. Every day as we labor, God's Spirit surrounds us, His messengers attend us, and the cloud of heavenly witnesses follows our lives with joy and pride. "I am come," He said, "that they might have life, and that they might have it more abundantly!" (John 10:10, KJV).

3. *Living*

"I hope you live until you die," a little boy told Dr. Norman Vincent Peale. Continuing to partake of life at its best, its challenges, its excitements, and even its disappointments is essential if we would keep looking up.

A former dean at Princeton University, Dr. Russell Wicks, once visited an old man at Mount Tom in Massachusetts. "I have an unusual view of the Berkshire mountains here," the man told Dr. Wicks. He pointed to four panes of glass in which the scene was the same, but the impression was different through each pane. The blue glass had the look of winter. The brown seemed like fall. The green gave the appearance of early springtime. And the red pane spoke of the glory of summer.

Our living can be like that. Various people look at life from different perspectives, depending on the "colored glass" of their attitudes. The pessimist sees only hopelessness and evil. The child of God gazes on the same troubled world, but sees life as it can be when it conforms to God's will. He does not despair, for he knows that God's plan is slowly being accomplished through him and circumstances.

Too many of our great philosophers peer through the "blue" pane of pessimism. In his latter years, Bertrand Russell was tinged with deep gloom: "Brief and powerless is a man's life," he wrote. "On him and all his race the slow, sure doom falls pitiless and dark. Blind to good and evil, reckless of destruction, omnipotent matter rolls on its relentless way. For man is condemned today to lose his dearest, tomorrow himself to pass through the gate of darkness . . ."

"Not so," says the Christian, quoting the Psalmist: "I had fainted, unless I had believed to see the goodness of the Lord in the land of the living" (Ps. 27:13, KJV).

In the 1920s, the Reverend Charles Sylvester Horne was returning to England from a successful evangelistic tour of Canada and the United States. He and his wife had visited some of the largest churches of both countries, and he had also delivered the Yale lectures for that year. He was now going home by ship, northeastward along the St. Lawrence River. Without warning, he dropped to the deck—dead.

When the ship arrived at Southampton, the captain (who had witnessed the whole episode) went to his own home pastor and asked to join the church; he now professed faith in Christ. The minister was pleased but surprised. "Why," he asked, "after so many years of my prayers are you now willing to join?" The captain related the story of Sylvester Horne's death, and then added, "When that man died on deck, I was only a few yards from him. Immediately, his wife knelt by his side and prayed in a quiet whisper, 'Dear Lord, thank You for letting us live such a full life of faith and joy together these many years!' "

Paul Tournier speaks of the exuberant life in this fashion: "The joy of living, of making an effort, of having a goal to aim at; the joy of moving a finger, of smelling a perfume, of looking at something, of hearing a voice, of learning something and loving someone . . . the pleasure of understanding something we did not understand before, of knowing what one did not know, the pleasure of the puzzle and its solution . . ." These, we know, are some of the joys of living.

Soren Kierkegaard, the great Danish theologian, adds his note to this thought: "The thing is to understand *myself*, to see what God really wishes *me* to do . . . to find the idea for which I can live and die!"

Almost every visitor in Florence seeks out Michaelangelo's statue of David, the shepherd lad. It is a masterpiece in marble.

But a hundred years or more before that artist's time, a magnificent block of Carrara marble had been brought to Florence by an unknown sculptor. He worked on it for a while, blocking out a figure he had in mind. Suddenly, he bungled his work by cutting a great slice out of the side. The stone had become useless to him, and he cast the marble aside.

There the piece of stone lay for a century until the trained eyes of Michaelangelo saw it. Immediately, he envisioned its possibilities. He began to outline, fashion, chisel, and carve. A majestic figure—the statue of David—soon stepped out of the stone, and even the other artist's mutilation had become part of the majesty of the new design.

Out of the ruin of a life or the hardships of aging, Jesus can take our every defect and fashion us into His own image.

4. *Dying*

As a person is born, he begins to die. Life is a constant struggle to maintain balance, to heal one's body and mind, to avoid fatal hazards, to grow and develop—not to shrink or decrease.

Martin Heidegger has put it thus: "Death is not an event which happens to man, but an event which he lives through from birth onward. From the moment he appears, man is on the point of dying. He is born and lives in the mortal mode. As soon as a man lives, he is old enough to die. . . . Death is a constituent of our being. Day after day, we live through our death. Man is, in his essence, a being-for-death. . . . Death teaches us that life is a value, but an incomplete value."

Many years ago, I witnessed the death of a beloved aunt. At first, she was terrified as death approached. But, as we read together from the great sustaining passages of Scripture (Ps. 23, John 14, 2 Cor. 5, etc.), a sense of peace flowed through her.

Finally, toward the end, she asked, "What is death like?" My mother, full of years and experience as well as spiritual insight, replied, "It's just like going to sleep, dear. You fall asleep here and wake up in His presence. It's very beautiful." She closed her eyes with a smile, and a few moments later slipped into eternity.

My friend Ted Engstrom, in his most recent book, says, "The fear of death causes us to clutch desperately at life . . . but Jesus has broken the chains of fear and dread and would have us open our 'clutching' hands as it were, and give to Him not only our lives, but also the moment of our death. . . . Anything He provides will be good. He is our Father, loving and caring for us as His children. . . . In the very act of entrusting our death to the Lord, we accept its inevitability—something each of us must do."

182

A friend of mine translates Matthew 16:25 thus: "Only when you are willing to let go with human life are you ready to hold onto life and meaningfully enjoy it."

We need to accept life in order to improve its quality. Taking an inventory of our life and correcting its course helps us stimulate new resolves and resources. The fear of death, if we allow it, can drain away such resources.

Kübler-Ross, a specialist in this area, writes, "It is the denial of death that is partially responsible for people living empty, purposeless lives; for when you live as if you'll live forever, it becomes easy to postpone the things you know that you must do. . . . In contrast, when you fully understand that each day you awaken could be the last one you have, you take the time *that day* to grow, to become more of who you really are, and to reach out to other human beings."

To find a meaningful goal toward the sunset of our lives is difficult for many, because they have used a shotgun approach to living. But if we look deeply enough, we will see unity in all our years—serving God. "That man is happiest," said Goethe, "who can reconcile the end of his life with its beginning." As we look back from our late fifties, our sixties or seventies, we appreciate a growing sense of completeness—a success, if Christ dwells within us. And as Christians, we realize afresh that the greatest of successes have been those moments of obedience to God.

5. *Rising*

"Eternal life," said one saint to me recently, "does not begin after death, but we start living it here and now. True, it is often masked by our daily business and duties. It is only as we touch death itself that we discover this truth." "Our Lord is not a God of the dead but of the living," said Jesus.

Christians are of all people the most blessed, because this new life is both here and now and also waits for us. God gives us His peace and joy as a foretaste of heaven. While the illnesses and regrets of this life weigh on us heavily, the underlying peace and glory ahead brightens our ongoing eternity. It becomes clearer and clearer that earthly death is a joy and a release. "To live is

Christ," said Paul, "and to die is gain." Or as the Psalmist puts it: "Even when walking through the dark valley of death, I will not be afraid, for You are close beside me, guarding and guiding all the way" (TLB).

Bodily resurrection is an essential part of our faith, for Christ's rising is the seal and proof of our salvation. The hope of our resurrection keeps us looking up to Jesus, the Author and Perfecter of our faith. When He promised to prepare a home in heaven for His children, He was not just feeding us fantasy, but a future, a real experience. As one elderly saint said to me many years ago, "Heaven is a beautiful place. And there I will hear Him telling me all the things that I have wondered about." Measure your relationship to Christ on the following pages.

184

Although our relationship to Jesus Christ is the most difficult dimension of life to measure, the following may help you partially gauge the immeasurable quotient:

	Yes	Some	No
1. Do you read and study the Scripture in some programmed way for at least 30 minutes a day?	___	___	___
2. Do you have a regular quiet hour daily when you pray and meditate on some devotional literature?	___	___	___
3. Do you gather with other Christians for worship and study at least once a week (church, Bible study, etc.)?	___	___	___
4. Do you belong to a group or class that requires systematic Bible study?	___	___	___
5. Have you attended workshops or retreats that can teach you how to pray and meditate better?	___	___	___
6. Do you feel you have a close relationship with Christ as your Lord and Savior?	___	___	___
7. Do you have a planned family time of devotion daily?	___	___	___
8. Do you spend time regularly in personal mission work, such as helping the poor, visiting the sick, comforting the heavy-hearted, and personal witnessing?	___	___	___
10. Do you serve your church in a regular way (the choir, a board, a committee, the Sunday school, etc.)?	___	___	___
Totals	___	___	___

If you wish to score yourself, give 10 for each "yes," 5 for each "some," and 0 for each "no." Most important of all is "practicing the presence of God." (This is such a personal and difficult area to probe that it is wholly between you and your Lord. These are only some of the ways that our faith might manifest itself.)

Index

Bibliography

Adler, Joan, *The Retirement Book*, New York, William Morrow & Co., Inc., 1975.

Bellak, Leopold, M.D., *The Best Years of Your Life*, New York, Atheneum Press, 1975.

Bolles, Richard N., *The Three Boxes of Life*, Berkeley, Calif., Ten Speed Press, 1978.

Buber, Martin, *I and Thou*, New York, Charles Scribners' Sons, 1970.

Clinebell, Howard, J. and Charlotte H., *The Intimate Marriage*, New York, Harper and Row Publishers, 1970.

Conway, Jim, *Men in Mid-Life Crisis*, Elgin, Ill., David C. Cook, 1978.

Cousins, Norman, *Anatomy of an Illness*, New York, W.W. Norton & Co., 1979.

Dangott, Lillian R. And Kalish, Richard A., *A Time to Enjoy* (The Pleasures of Aging), Englewood Cliffs, N.J., Prentice-Hall, Inc., 1979.

Dayton, Edward R., and Engstrom, Ted. W., *Strategy for Leadership*, Old Tappan, N.J., Fleming H. Revell Co., 1979.

Dyer, Wayne W., *Pulling Your Own Strings*, New York, Avon Press, 1977.

Engstrom, Ted. W., *The Most Important Thing a Man Needs to Know About the Rest of His Life*, Old Tappan, N.J., Fleming H. Revell, 1981.

Erikson, Erik, Ed., *Adulthood*, New York, W.W. Norton & Co., Inc., 1978.

Freedman, Jonathan L., *Happy People*, New York, Harcourt Brace Jovanovich, 1978.

Friedman, Meyer, M.D., and Rosenman, Ray H., M.D., *Type A Behavior and Your Heart*, New York, Fawcett Columbinett, 1974.

Gould, Roger L., M.D., *Transformations*, New York, Simon & Schuster, 1978.

Gubrium, Jaber F., *Time, Roles and Self in Old Age*, New York, Human Sciences, 1979.

Hansen, Percy M., *Never Too Late to Be Young*, New York, Frederick Fell, Inc., 1966.

Hutschnecker, Arnold A., M.D., *The Will to Live*, New York, Thomas Crowell, 1951.

Jacobs, Ruth Harriet, *Life After Youth*, Boston, Beacon Press, 1975.

Jung, Carl G., *Modern Man in Search of a Soul*, New York, Harcourt Brace and World, Inc., 1933.

Kanin, Garson, *It Takes a Long Time to Become Young*, New York, Doubleday & Co., Inc. 1978.

Kordel, Gaylord, *You're Younger Than You Think*, New York, Fawcett Popular Library, 1976.

Kübler-Ross, Elisabeth, *On Death and Dying*, New York, Macmillan Publishing Co., 1969.

Lakein, Alan, *How to Get Control of Your Time and Life*, New York, New American Library, A Signet Book, 1973.

Landers, Ann, *The Ann Landers Encyclopedia A to Z*, New York, Doubleday & Co., Inc. 1978.

May, Rollo, *Man's Search for Himself*, New York, The New American Library, Inc., 1967.

McQuade, Walter, and Aikman, Anne, *Longevity Factor*, New York, Simon & Schuster, 1979.

Miller, Gordon P., *Life Choices*, New York, Thomas Crowell Publishers, 1978.

Nudel, Adele, *For the Woman Over Fifty*, New York, Avon Books, 1978.

Ortlund, Ray and Anne, *The Best Half of Life*, Glendale, Calif., Regal Books, 1976.

Otte, Elmer, *Retirement Rehearsal Guidebook*, Indianapolis, Editorial Inc., 1971.

Peterson, James A. and Payne, Barbara, *Love in the Later Years*, New York, Association Press, 1975.

Pitkin, Walter P., Jr., *Life Begins at Fifty*, New York, Simon and Schuster, 1965.

Pruner, Morton, *Getting the Most out of Your Fifties*, New York, Crown Publishers, Inc., 1977.

Pruner, Morton, *To the Good Long Life*, New York, Universe Books, 1974.

Scarf, Maggie, *Unfinished Business*, 1980, Garden City, N.Y., Doubleday & Co., 1980.

Schwartz, David J., Ph.D., *The Magic of Thinking Big*, N.Y., Simon & Schuster, 1959.

Seskin, Jane, *More Than Mere Survival*, New York, Newsweek Books, 1980.

Sheehy, Gail, *Passages*, New York, E. P. Dutton, 1976.

Sheehy, Gail, *Pathfinders*, New York, William Morrow, Inc., 1981.

Smith, Bert Kruger, *Aging in America*, Boston, Beacon Press, 1973.

Tournier, Paul, *The Adventure of Living*, New York, Harper and Row, 1965.

Tournier, Paul, *Learn to Grow Old*, New York, Harper and Row, 1972.

Tournier, Paul, *The Meaning of Persons*, New York, Harper and Row, 1957.

Uris, Auren, *Over 50*, Radnor, Pa., Chilton Books Co., 1979.

Van Tassel, David D., Ed., *Aging, Death and the Completion of Being*, Philadelphia University of Pennsylvania Press, 1979.

Weinstein, Grace W., *Life Plans* (Looking Forward to Retirement), New York, Holt, Rinehart and Winston, 1979.

Wright, Norman, *An Answer to Worry and Anxiety*, Irvine, Cal., Harvest House, 1976.